WHAT THEY'RE SAYING ABOUT

the INSIGHTS COLLECTION
Insights from the Engine Room

"Tony has seen more of the music industry from the inside than almost anyone else I know. Working for various record companies, his own promotional business and in artist management has given him a deep insight into the machinations of the music business. His success stories are many but just ask any member of U2 about Tony and they will tell you of the crucial role he played in getting them heard around the UK. More than this though, he is a man who loves music and that's what has driven him more than anything else."

Mark Radcliffe

BBC Radio 2 Presenter and author.

"Tony has been one of the most talented, remarkable and personable people I have ever encountered. He is an individual of exceptional capabilities and a unique player in the field of regional promotion"

Michael Lippman

Manager of Matchbox Twenty, George Michael

"Tony has taken his unique ability to look in retrospect at his experience from the music industry and create practical business lessons that can applied by any entrepreneur or corporate leader. He explains the lessons in a way that not only resonates with today's business challenges but is a storyteller whose vignettes you will not soon forget."

Thomas W. Nash

Chairman and CEO Xalles Ltd.

"Tony invented the concept of regional promotion that equated the power of music and the quality of voice for hip labels and their talented new artists and did imaginative and successful work in the heartland when all music companies clung to the London media. I was so pleased he wrote a book as someone would now have to edit him!"

Ray Cooper

Zama Management, Former President Virgin Records US

"Tony Michaelides is a legend and as Tony gave me my first job in the music industry he'll always be a legend to me. His enthusiasm for plugging and life in general is contagious and reading his stories kept me entertained from cover to cover!"

Manager of Coldplay 2002 – 2006

Estelle Wilkinson

"Tony did my PR for years then was my manager for a while with Revenge. I remember going to a record company planning meeting with him shortly after we'd arrived in America where the meeting dragged on for ages. He didn't say much, he seemed deep in thought, very serious. When the meeting finally wrapped up I turned to him and said "What do you think, Tony?" "ZZZZzzzz" he said.............PURE CLASS!"

Peter Hook, Bassist

Joy Division and New Order

"What I like best of all is Tony's sheer, unadulterated bloody minded love of music of music and life, which comes across with gusto. And also his constant thankfulness for being able to live out a hobby for a career."

Mark Hodkinson

The London Times

"I only wish we could all have a tiny Tony around to whisper in our ears some of his inspirational stories to remind us not to take ourselves quite so seriously. We could learn a valuable lesson from his experiences and realize that making decisions on instinct can sometimes be far more rewarding than relying on the same old corporate wave of feast to famine. Never has the time been so right for riding Tony's mantra on how to harness the wave and win."

Avril Somerville

Management and Training Specialist

"Tony has taken the lessons learned from a lifetime inside the rock machine and constructed a new way of fine tuning business practice. The stars he has worked with can now be your inspirational motivators."

Colin Somerville

Journalist Scotland On Sunday, Presenter BBC Radio Scotland

the INSIGHTS
COLLECTION
Insights from the Engine Room

LESSONS LEARNED FROM ROCK AND ROLL

TONY MICHAELIDES
Foreword by Dr. David Robert Penn, Ph. D.

JANSON
MEDIA GROUP

THE INSIGHTS COLLECTION
INSIGHTS FROM THE ENGINE ROOM:
Lessons Learned from Rock and Roll
©2009 Tony Michaelides
Foreword by David Robert Penn, Ph. D.
Janson Media, First Edition
Editor: Bobbi Janson (jansonmedia.com)
Cover Design: Darrin Guilbeau (siliconadvantage.com)
Cover Photo: Craig Carreno (thecarrenogallery.com)
Photo Credits: Kevin Cummins and Tony Michaelides

Available wherever books are sold. Special case-quantity discounts are available to corporations and educational institutions. All premium and marketing inquiries will be considered. Please contact us at: *info@insightscollection.com.*

Library of Congress Cataloging-in-Publication Data:
      Insights From the Engine Room: Lessons Learned from Rock and Roll /Tony
      Michaelides   p. cm. Current PPD 2009 Acid-free Paper

1. Music—Trade—Vocational Guidance—United States
2. Music—Promotion—Managing—UK
I. Title   II. Michaelides, Tony

LCCN: 2009937324
ISBN: 1-889131-81-4   ISBN: 9781889131818
Manufactured in the United States of America
Published simultaneously in Canada and the UK
10 9 8 7 6 5 4 3 2 1

For Jess and Joe

The future belongs to those who believe

in the beauty of their dreams.

—Eleanor Roosevelt

and for my mother

who taught me the true values of life.

To Russell,

Keep on Rockin'

all the best

Dec 2013

TABLE OF CONTENTS

*Bruce Springsteen
Hammersmith Palais
19 June 1981*

*Ray Cooper (from his Transatlantic
days, later became president of Virgin
Records)*

*The man responsible for all the
mayhem.... gave me my first job
in the music industry 1974*

*L to R, The Edge, Bono, (U2)
and Tony the Burger Guy*

*You can see from early on in their
career, U2 always had that hunger....*

*Bono, Live onstage
Manchester Apollo 1983*

*Tony Michaelides and daughter, Jess, in first Promotion Office
Representing artists' for Island and A & M Records 1980*

*L to R, Mike Rutherford, Tony Michaelides, Phil Collins
Outside Radio City Radio Station, Liverpool during Genesis 'Duke' Tour 1980*

Family Pass, for U2's Homecoming Gig,
14 August 1983, Phoenix Park, Dublin

Free Trade Hall Ticket

Tony with
The Edge
(U2)

Larry Mullen (drummer U2)
teaching my daughter Jess to
Stage-dive, May 1982

Gateshead, Newcastle, England 1982

The Hardrock—
now a home improvement center

The late great John Peel,
BBC Radio DJ

Island Records, 22 St. Peters Square, London

Free Trade Hall '69
Manchester, UK

Belle Vue
Manchester, UK

Where Tony met Led Zeppelin backstage
A moment that changed his life... .

FOREWORD

Insights from the Engine Room is a wonderful story about Tony Michaelides' life on the road. Tony has worked with some of the music industry's greatest talents. The performers, managers, and producers include Simon Cowell, U2, David Bowie, Whitney Houston, Matchbox Twenty, Paul McGuiness, Michael Lippman, Virgin Records former president Ray Cooper and many more. As to be expected, Tony as a Brit, is full of wit. His wit reminds us to live our lives with humor and passion and let the music roll off our tongues to guide us in other areas of our lives.

Management helps us plan for personal goals. These goals help us establish our life mission regarding our family, career, health, faith, finances, and future and most of all to have fun. Tony is a life and management coach with incredible relationship skills gained from his life and PR career. He is worthy of a great book and you are worthy of his ongoing coaching and speaking experiences that I encourage you to consider. You will certainly have fun getting to know the person behind the talent. He is the closest many of us will come to enjoying the celebrity lifestyle. Get to know Tony and apply his philosophy to help you.

In my life, I've been blessed by my faith, family, and an education that took me to Bryant, Harvard, and Northcentral University to complete studies in business, communications, psychology and management. I've had the joy of transforming organizations into multi-million dollar producing corporations through visionary leadership. I've had fun helping diverse children reach their potential and travelling extensively. I'm working on managing my life through health and financial goals. With a current career in academia as a university dean and professor, my future and your future are what we make of it and how we apply life's lessons. Now, I'm blessed to have Tony as a friend. He reminds me to live a full life. I came to know Tony through mutual friends. Nick DiCosola is a talented, Berklee educated musician with strong leadership skills that tell us he will reach his dreams and achieve music and leadership milestones. Carolyn Quintin, a management consultant, is a kind soul and talented leader. She reminds me that compassion and listening are great traits to help each other and to achieve one's truest creative passion.

Enjoy this book, take time to apply its lessons to your life. Play some music and let the melody of the REWINDS at the end of each chapter help advance your goals. We hope our insights through the fun of rock and roll and a life of leadership will guide you.

For rockin' Robin, *you are my rock and funny valentine.* For Audrey Ruth, my curly girly, *you are a beautiful leader and model.* For Jack Vito, my buddy, *you are a strong, intelligent soul.* For Arthur James, my special friend, *you are a soft-spoken, gentle artist.* For Mom and Papa, *thanks for the special anniversary date we all share.* For Gram, my mentor, *you are the epitome of grace, friendship and business savvy.*

DR. David Robert Penn, Ph.D.
Dean of Strayer University

INTRODUCTION

Write a book!

Now, why on earth would I do that? I inquired.

It seemed bizarre. After all, who would want to buy a book that I'd written? Oddly enough it wasn't just some rambling idiot telling me to write a book—a few had started to mention it—then came the comforting words.

Nowadays everyone writes a book,
all sorts of tossers write books.

Okay, so now I was a tosser. Ego shattered, I began warming to the idea. Maybe I SHOULD write a book. But what book? More pensive moments, it still wasn't enough. I want to write a book that I'd read. I want it to include stories, be entertaining and I want it to have humour. I want there to be something practical that people could gain from the stories. I want them to benefit and learn as I had learned from the people I had worked with.

Insights From The Engine Room is about the music industry. It's about the people I met along the way. It's about teaching some things and learning from others who stared at failure and learned how to handle success. It's about where they came from and where they went and what happened to them in between. It's about how they became who they are. It's about real people and it's littered with real stories.

It's a book about the world I grew up in, first as a fan—until I was given the chance to make a living from it. It was the job I never expected but one I would never let go. It was an opportunity and it was one hell of an adventure. It was this pilgrim's progress. It was the journey I took with the people I met in the places I went to. It was our place and it was our time.

You have to have lived it and you have to have worked it. You had to spend every day totally absorbed in it. To do that you had to love it and I did love it, all of it. Maybe when I started I thought it might be a brief affair, a passing fling. But the passion hits hard and it pulled me in for the long haul.

If you were after the warts n' all tell tale, I'm afraid this isn't it. There's more than enough of that in the media-crazed world we live in. The people who taught me were far more interesting and brought much greater value. They are the *real* of reality and the *stars* of star-makers. It's a book any of us could have written but it's my book. It's about my experiences and it's my story. You won't hear all of the stories as there are far too many but the ones I'll share will help you to believe there is a way for the music industry to survive. After all who would want to discredit Elvis, Hank and Woody?

Rock and roll is about heroes. Somewhere along the way we lost sight of that. Writing this was my catharsis, my way to try and help find them again and to wonder why a generation growing up never had them to miss them. What a shame. When David Bowie told us *We can be heroes just for one day….* he meant it. He wanted us to dream.

I'm grateful I took the time out to listen to those who told me right then *write a book!* Thanks for being louder than me, for once. And as with most things I couldn't have done it without my team of trusted confidants, the ones who'd kick me when I wasn't even down!

Arise Sir Darrin, the Baird of New Orleans who took me into his techno tee-pee and told me all the ways we could publicize and promote. He designed, designated and dedicated his time and energy. He got it, all of it from the get go. He assembled a formidable team of creative people with ideas and vision who were an inspiration to me. From the bottom of my page, I thank him.

Thank you Erin for a cover I'm truly proud to put my name on. And who could forget Brian from Digital Media Services of Florida and the hours he spent teaching me how computers did much more than e-mails. His direction and guidance gave me the incentive to create the sound and vision to compliment the stories and lessons.

Arise too, Dr. D, thank you for the support and encouragement in getting this show on the road. The Penn is mightier than the sword. Write on! And not forgetting Peter for the beignets and original ideas on how we should roll out this stone (me.) Together with Michelle I was dusted and trusted, groomed and bloomed and encouraged to bring forth the tales of old. Well not that old! Thank you all for the friendship and guidance.

To Diana and Sally, for the belief they had and the patience to listen; they were there from the beginning and without that, I may have talked about writing a book but not actually written one. Finally, to Nick for introducing me to some great people. Thank you all for the friendship and guidance. And of course, the two shining stars in my galaxy who got the whole of the previous page, now go to your room.

Thank you Janson Media Group, publishers with passion who aided and abetted admirably where others might have interfered. I'm glad we're on the same page. I still can't believe you all were happy to work with such a clown. Nevertheless I love the lot of you.

And finally I'd like to thank me for taking the time to spend time with myself and do this. I never knew I had it in me (okay, I lied).

And so it came to pass I got my book and I got it how I wanted it. These are the *Insights From The Engine Room* and some of the things that happened along the way.

I hope you enjoy the stories and find insights of help.
If you do then you made my day, punk.
And if you don't…. shit happens.

CHAPTER 1

ALL THIS ACCORDING TO ME

LET THE JOURNEY BEGIN

Writing is a struggle against silence.

—*Carlos Fuentes*

Decision made, I was now officially writing a book. So what now? Is there a book protocol? Should I do things a certain way? I need to write a book but I need to write a proper book, a book with substance. I think I can do that. In fact, I know I can. I can be proper.

A momentary lapse of reason

I started to think, *I'll write a book but I won't tell anyone about it.* My reasoning here was that if I've got a book out then everyone's going to expect me to send them a free copy. Where's the sense in that? I'll be spending all day going backwards and forwards to the post office mailing them out and it'll cost me a small fortune. This was getting ridiculous—I'm a PR guy and I want to write a book but not tell anyone about it?

If I write a book it would get me out of the house more and I like talking and I like writing. I'm bound to like this! Result, I've decided to do it. I can promote it myself, I like that too. Now it's all starting to make sense. I started to quietly mention it to more friends and they all said, *Perfect, just the job!* Now I had to write a book so that I could talk about writing a book.

Talk less, write more

I became suspicious of my friend's intentions. Was this some sort of master plan? If I was kept busy maybe they were thinking they wouldn't have to listen to me! What kind of friends are these? This was getting ludicrous. I was looking for people to blame. Okay, I'll write a book and if no one buys it I'll blame them. It's my account of my book and I'll be unaccountable. I was happy again.

Wherever there's an excuse, there's always a solution

I began dreaming it up in my head and I was getting a lot of encouraging feedback from my blog. This started me writing about life and the things that happen in life. Now here was my opportunity to shout louder. I'm on the rooftops hollering, *WHAT NEXT?*

What a great way to spread the word, tweeting. I needed to shout louder still. A book, that's it! By now I'd convinced myself it was my idea, a stroke of pure genius and genius is worthy of book writing. I'll do it.

Blogging had been fun. We'd become close, me and blog. It felt like two old men in a pub shouting across the room to each other but in cyberspace. I was in the web-pub and I was being random! Makes sense, actually.

Blogging is ranting, ranting is random and random is me. Now there was a reason. I had a purpose. I could blog my way through an entire book—just blogging and ranting until I was out of blog roll.

Writing for a reason

It did have to have a purpose and be of value though. It's about what I learned in life and what thirty years in the music industry taught me. I want you to see the mistakes these people made along with the opportunities that came their way, the pivotal moments that had both motivated and inspired me. I want you to see that no matter who you are, shit happens! We all live and I wanted to share my life with you. I started to make some notes, relive some of those wonderful experiences. I started to think back on those wonderful experiences. Wow, I'm going to enjoy writing this. I know me and I know this is what I want to do. I'm grateful to have the opportunity to pass it on.

I definitely was on a mission now. How long should it be and what's it about? What will I call it? I'd made the decision though, I'm writing a book! I started to think about the cover. Agreed, we need one. It should have me on the cover in a Superhero costume. Maybe 'Brit-man?' I scribbled some more notes and identified the things I wanted to cover. There was too much—time to prioritize. There will definitely be more. I'll be hungry like the wolf. What wolf? It has to begin at the beginning but I know once I start I won't want it to end. It has to introduce me from my childhood to my adulthood but we need to cover my in-between-hood because my in-between-hood was good.

You need to know who I am and where I came from to understand why I'm writing this. You need to get inside my head—well, maybe not. And then where I'm going, possibly? Pass…. I've no clue! We'll cover several topics and see where we end up. There will be stories and lessons and when we arrive at the end we'll begin again, with more lessons and more stories from more books. It's a journey that feels right, right now. I could have done it years ago but I didn't and anyway it's none of your business. I'm making a new business from my old business so we can have a business to share, and make it your business. While fiction is good, fact is gold. If I wasn't writing it, I'd be reading it but I couldn't read it because I hadn't written it, yet. So I did! Once I'd made up my mind I was going to do this, I HAD to do it. I had to make it my life's mission. Too much was inside waiting to come out and now, with the help and encouragement of others, here it is. The ultimate test: *Why expect anyone to be interested in reading something that you wouldn't want to read yourself?*

**Wisdom is not a product of schooling but the
lifelong attempt to acquire it.**
—Albert Einstein

I started scribbling and started to become excited. To some it's a book. For me it's really a diary, a perfect way to remember those times and to relive some of those moments. It's to help me understand some of the lessons that the music business taught me and about how vital those lessons were. Even though they're lessons I learned from rock and roll, they apply to us all. They are about real life.

It was also a time to be honest with myself, accept the rollercoaster of a life I'd had, sit down and decide on the bits worth telling. It was a time for me to appreciate the opportunity I had been given to make a living from a hobby. Music came into my life and it never really left. Now, another opportunity presents itself and it's the desire to give something back. It's my indulgence and it's my reward. It's my chance to make it your chance and to help you see what happens to people we know, as well those we don't. It's what you learn from the experience that makes the difference.

To love your job is unusual because to some it's just work. It's something people come to and go away from and that's where it stays, in the workplace. To me it never felt like work. It was like being given the keys to the sweet shop and told to wander around and pick the ones you liked. Nowadays students have the luxury of studying what we made up as we went along. They are not growing up in the climate we did, whereby if you screwed up, you got a second chance. We were allowed to make mistakes and we were judged on how we recovered from them.

Wisdom comes from questions, not from answers

We were prepared to take chances and to look for opportunities. It made us challenge questions and allowed us to learn from answers. Whatever wisdom came from that probably took years to fully appreciate. What I do know is that it taught me something everyday and to be able to pass that on to others is a gift. If you want to learn then you always want to learn; for me, there's rarely a day goes by where I don't find something out. It might be in a newspaper, on the web or from someone I meet. It might not change my world but at least I'll allow myself the chance to find out.

It's my work, he'd say and I do it for pay.
And when it's over I'd just as soon go on my way.
—Bob Dylan

Do it your way; make it your own was the first lesson I ever learned and it was the one lesson I gave everyone who ever worked for me. I wanted people to make their own mistakes because I wanted them to learn from those mistakes. I wanted to instill that confidence in them the way others had done with me, to do it exactly the way *they* thought it should be done and whatever happened didn't matter. We would always find a way through. I was always there to help.

Where you go depends on how you begin

The corporate culture of record companies today doesn't allow for the mavericks and the gunslingers, the moguls and the mentors. You get it wrong and you're out. There's no Chris Blackwells or Ahmet Erteguns encouraging you to have a go. These are the people who would support you, whether you were an artist or a member of staff. They had the utmost belief in what they did and they shared that belief with everyone, every day. It was infectious. Their belief becomes your belief—you believe in them and they believe in you. It was never us against them.

We were blessed with a media as hungry as we were to showcase that talent. We gave and we gratefully accepted and we all shared in each other's successes. And we had fun, fun, fun. We cared enough to believe in the dream. Rock and roll is here to stay, if we just let it.

CHAPTER 2

SO THE TITLE THEN

INSIGHTS FROM THE ENGINE ROOM

I have the simplest of taste.

I'm always satisfied with the best.

—Oscar Wilde

My original intention was to call this, *Insights from The Engine Room*. I loved the title but nobody knew what it meant except me and why would I want to write a book for me to know what I already knew? Once I wrote the book I felt I'd only just begun. This was an iceberg and I barely tipped it. By the time I edited stuff out and I was looking at the 'cutting room floor' there were many of the topics I wanted to have the opportunity to revisit. There were more stories to tell and even more lessons to learn. They come from Rock and Roll but they end up in everyday life. The *Insights Collection's* first born is here in *Insights from the Engine Room*. Yes I know you don't know what the *Engine Room* is so sit back, relax and I'll tell you. That way we'll all know and the world will be a happier place.

Hey Mr. Tambourine Man, play a song for me

Well, *Insights....* is exactly that, it's the sights from the inside. It's about the people behind the scenes, the creative infrastructure of the music business. It's about the people you don't often get to hear about as well as those you do. The Engine Room is the creative cog in the machine and that machine is the music business.

The mechanics that drive the machine

In the Engine Room are the managers and the promoters, the producers and the publicists and of course, the artists. You'll also find the collaborators who work tirelessly at pulling all the strands together by combining their individual and collective talents. The PR's are there too building and creating the image, together with the publicists planning the publicity.

There are those managing the creativity of the artist while also creatively managing those around them. Managing creativity and creative management are not the same and as such, must be approached differently. If you get it right you let the art exist, and if you don't—you're letting the art exit!

Begin the adventure from where you first set sail

Each experience, whether it's an opportunity or a risk, grooms you for the next. With every mistake comes the opportunity to get it right. I learned a lot from a whole bunch of people and I'm going to share some of those experiences with you. I'll let you see how those you might admire from a distance can be a little closer linked to what you do today, but more importantly what you do tomorrow.

We'll look at what happened to some of those people at defining moments in their careers, how some of their toughest challenges became their greatest opportunities. And we'll see risk and collaboration helping to dictate the way you do things.

If you believe it enough it won't be hard to convince others

It's important to remember that Bono and his band of merry men were once upon a time a bunch of little Irish kids craving a stab at the limelight. They had such a tremendous belief in themselves they felt it their mission to get others to believe in them. There is so much to learn from this one band alone, how they took every risk and made every mistake to remain innovative throughout their journey.

Everyday pleasures can be every day treasures

As a thirteen year old there was nothing I wanted more than to be a professional footballer and to grace the hallowed turf of Old Trafford, The Theatre of Dreams, home of Manchester United. I'd practice for hours behind the library where I lived (not that I lived in the library) longing for the day when the phone would ring and it would be Archie Mc Whoever (they're all called Archie) summoning me to my trial.

It was acre upon acre of pure pasture, free of dog poop and discarded syringes. Lush with velvet grass that was as green as envy. Total bliss! We didn't even need to put our jumpers down as posts as we had the real thing. There were no nets but fabulous white goalposts were painted twice a year. They even had stanchions.

This was amateur football at its finest and maybe I was one of amateur's finest footballers. I was happy to believe it. I was practicing free kicks and bending them before Beckham, he was the merest twinkle in his mother's eye. Quite why I have no clue. I ended up playing centre half and never took another. Easier than practicing to tackle an imaginary forward I suppose, though it still doesn't explain me taking up goalkeeping when I played with my brother, Mike.

Getting down and dirty

Playing out on that field, I'd come home bruised and battered but deliriously happy that I'd tipped one of my brother's pile drivers over the bar. (Apologies if we get lost in translation, a pile-driver being the speed of a traveling football and no resemblance whatsoever to the removal of less than pleasant hemorrhoids).

I thought Michael showed real potential, possibly the next George Best. Sadly the resemblance ended with the haircut and his developing taste for beer, women and gambling. I was to later discover that he'd aim his free kicks high above the largest muddiest (only) puddle, knowing that if I saved them I'd come crashing down and get covered in crap. Drenched from head to toe nothing else mattered. I was a happy, little urchin. I could hear the roar of the crowd, see them waving their scarves and chanting my name! I would come home, bath, go straight to bed and dream that one day I would be a professional footballer and play for Manchester United—or would I?

If you can dream it, then you can dream of doing it

Weekends it was football, football and more football. I was playing two games on a Saturday, one in the morning, and one in the afternoon. It was an hour's drive between them and no time to shower but enough time for the mud on my legs to go crusty. I was then able to flick it off, change and be ready for my next game.

Many a time I'd get there and have to run on to the pitch fifteen minutes into the game. The following morning it was up again and off to play another game. Growing up in the north of England in the '60s every boy's childhood dream was to be a footballer. You played every opportunity you got. It was why we were put on this earth.

The summer of love

Born in 1953, I was the perfect age for the arrival of the *Summer of Love*. I baby boomed and lapped it up. It was the dawning of the hippy and love was in the air. We were all warned 'be sure to wear some flowers in your hair' so shaving heads was not cool. It was flowers, beads and more flowers. The girls looked equally as pretty. I need to thank my mother for conceiving when she did (good timing there, mum)

They even crowned a queen for me the year I was born and trooped the color on my first birthday. Before long I sensed the need for regalia, I needed to be crowned and not for one day. I needed for find something to satisfy what it was I didn't know that I wanted to do! I needed to explore my passion which was music but what was that going to be?

Growing up and growing into music

Growing up in the 60s was both a pleasure and a passion. Sorry, I can't give you any stories about a tough upbringing because there wasn't one. I was a happy child, still am. There were no stories about my dad leaving home when I was three, my mum having four jobs, seven of us sleeping in the same room. We never starved, always had clothes that were our own and never needed to be reliant on the neighbor's cast offs.

On the contrary I have very fond memories of growing up, first as a passionate Manchester United fan until seduced by Roger McGuinn's (the Byrds) twelve string Rickenbacker when Mr. Tambourine played a song for me. Every jingle jangle morning I would come following him. He was my piper playing my tune. I was twelve.

The next few years never really ended. So many bands with so much to say and play and the type of education you could only dream about. It was music at its very finest and it set unbelievable standards for those who would follow.

Music can change the world
because it can change people.
—Bono

I was smitten by a whole youth culture driven by the most incredible movement of music from both sides of the Atlantic, The Byrds, Bob Dylan, Neil Young, Pink Floyd and Led Zeppelin. It left a lasting impression on me. Everything I did, from the friends I had to the places I went, all revolved around music. Could life get any better? Miraculously it did and very quickly. At fifteen all I wanted was to be a rock and roll star, and I think around eighteen-years old I started to grow up. I played bass in a band, badly but as I lived in the house where we rehearsed it was easy to see how I landed the job. My mum helped me keep it though, a calculated ploy I'm convinced. She'd always bring us freshly baked scones after the first five numbers. When that ended my rise to rock stardom was over, or was it? I tried my hand at managing the band, but managing what? We weren't doing any gigs and there wasn't a multi-million dollar record deal on the table, so the job wasn't too demanding. Still, it kept me in the music business.

The man with all the music

Every moment of every day I would listen to music. The late great John Peel, arguably the most influential DJ ever to come out of the UK had a show on Radio London at the time called *The Perfumed Garden*. It would be where I first heard so much of the music I grew to love. Peel's uniquely dry sense of humor matched by a plethora of bands with the most ridiculous names made the show compulsive listening for every teenager. You can blame him for leaving so many of us penniless, with all our allowances spent on buying records. Well that and going to gigs.

Peel appeal

John Peel remains an icon, a great unsung hero of our time. There was very little that passed by his turntable, at least nothing that mattered. He was instrumental in a whole generation discovering the music that would change our lives. You knew if there were any great new bands coming out—you'd hear them on Peel. If I couldn't be a rock star then maybe I could be Peel? I'd never considered that but twenty years later I found myself on the radio playing new bands alongside those timeless classics I grew up on. Peel I wasn't but I have to say I loved doing it. I thought it might last a couple of weeks, possibly a month? It lasted thirteen years! The bands were my heroes, I wanted to play like them but I was crap. There was never a chance of being a player but it didn't matter; it was the music that kept my attention and made me happy. No matter my own musical failings,

I still needed my heroes. Music created stars, stars had dreams and rock and roll fulfilled those dreams. But we had dreams too. Music had so much to do with everything you did, where you went, who you went there with, who you dated and who you hated. Love may have made the world go round but music was most definitely feeding it. If music be the food of love then call me a fat bastard!

Memories made of hits

I never kept a diary. I didn't need to. I could trace most major events in my life to the records that were released. I know what music was played at wedding(s), what I was listening to at school and in what year, what was playing in the refectory at my college, where I was when I first heard Dylan, Bowie, Hendrix and Led Zeppelin. I even know the exact dates I bought my records because I would write it on the top right hand corner of the sleeve. Ask me about David Bowie and Ziggy Stardust and The Spiders from Mars at The *Hard Rock Cafe* in Manchester, Sunday September 3rd 1972 and I'm there! I can tell you where I stood, who I went with, who I saw there and how I got there, the date, the price of the ticket and I could probably list most of the set. We have the internet for that now so I suppose I'd be able tell you the whole of the set.

Where were you when

I remember turning down Bob Dylan's *Positively 4th Street* on the jukebox when the news came on that they'd caught The Yorkshire Ripper. Or listening to John Lennon's *Instant Karma* while driving to work the morning Mark Chapman blasted a part of our youth away. It was the first time in my life I felt real hatred, and thankfully the last. Music played a huge part in absolutely everything you did. It was always the music that took you back to a specific time and a place and usually with a person. You can't say that about a sport, be it a goal or a race won. Only with music—it's permanently etched in your memory. I didn't need much imagination to dispose of my disposable income!

One Stop Records was situated on the approach road to Piccadilly Railway Station in Manchester, in the North of England. Every Saturday I would get the 9 o'clock train from Gatley and travel the five stops to the city. I'd be in the store at 9:28 am prompt.

It was hard waiting the few days between the music papers coming out and going to the record store. At school I'd be caught staring out of the window but I was young and I needed my windows. There were dreams outside every one. I'd get off the train, race down the platform and straight to the store where they'd have the latest releases ready for me to hear. I would spend the next few hours in the listening booths, never leaving without two shiny new albums and a satisfied smile across my face.

The train ride home seemed like forever and I was always greeted by the same miserable look on the same ticket collector's face. I'm sure he thought I'd been in the city for something vaguely illicit. I could never understand that whatever the weather, he had a face like a soiled bedpan.

Fortunately life was never as bad as the look on his Saturday Afternoon face. I'd usually sprint from the railway station back to my home and then it was eat, bath and straight 'round to one of my friend's houses to see what they'd bought, secretly hoping we hadn't duplicated. Weekends were perfect and as a fan, I would take my place. We all had to have dreams and I always was a dreamer.

Life's defining moments

Pivotal moments—so let's pivot! It was 1969 and too many groups were too good and even if they were bad they were never that bad. Pocket money was spent on going to gigs, whether they were concerts, small clubs or benefit shows in holes where you sat crossed legged on the floor. Incense filled the air. Okay, we pretended it was incense. You saw or heard very little but at least you were there, man!

Then there were the all-nighters at the Pavilion Gardens in Buxton, provided you didn't mind waiting five hours to go to the bathroom. Every time I needed to go, you could guarantee there'd be someone half way through a drum solo. You couldn't bear the humiliation of being stared at as you shuffled along the row and if you succumbed through necessity it was equivalent to a public flogging. People grunted and groaned refusing to move their legs to let you pass. You were made to feel like the rock leper.

No point crying over split Cream

I remember crying when Cream split up because I never got to see them play and I vowed I would never let this happen again. If I loved a band I had to see them live because one day they'd be gone. By now I was a grown man and couldn't risk bursting in tears every time someone split up. Surely this couldn't be true, I would see Eric Clapton again—wouldn't I? Music really started to impact me by age thirteen. After hearing Mr. Tambourine the previous year, it was Cream that catapulted me to music heaven and the point of no return. I'd been bitten.

Manna from heaven

Then along came Led Zeppelin. They were playing the Free Trade Hall, Manchester, June 1969 and my friend Ken had managed to get us some tickets. It was there and then I gave him the name Sir Kenneth to which he proudly answers to this day. I could barely contain myself with the excitement, Led Zeppelin in my home town and just prior to world domination. I had the type of seat a corporate CEO would have mortgaged his yacht for, so near the front I could watch Jimmy Page grimace and admire every Robert Plant gyration. I could smell the sweat off Bonzo as he destroyed his drums and feel John Paul Jones' bass creep up my leg and into my belly.

This was rock heaven. If the bass ever got too heavy and made me sick it was comforting knowing it was rock puke. After the show we waited around and asked the old bloke in the foyer (I think they call them security now) if we could take a couple of posters down from the wall. He politely obliged and there we stood with two glorious Zeppelin posters, the ones with the orange Zeppelin on the cover. They didn't sell merchandise back then so the masterpiece I had before me was about to become a priceless rarity and worth a small fortune. I got divorced, from wife and poster and the rest is history, or it could have been. I bid farewell to my retirement fund and my poster pension.

Hall of Fame

We sneaked back in the empty auditorium and watched as the roadies packed up the equipment. Now this was rock and roll. This was serious. The Marshall 4x12 speaker stacks were vast and plenty, rising high above the stage. What I wouldn't have done just to touch them, even if one could just fall over and land on me.

Oh, for the blood of Zeppelin! Just watching the roadies pack up would have been more than enough for us.

Suddenly out of nowhere Robert Plant appeared, leaned down and nodded at us, *Want me to sign those for you, fellahs?*—he asked. As if? I secretly kept calm wanting to make him feel the fledgling pop star. No sooner were we admiring his autograph than he waved us over to the stage door. *Over here lads*, he beckoned. I was beckoned beyond belief, now he was asking us if we wanted to meet the other guys. PLEEEEEEEEEASE, pinch me again. Is this really happening?

Dazed and confused

I looked at Ken and he looked at me. We both looked at Robert (by now he was Robert.) There was a lot of looking going on. I shuffled and wriggled in my Levis to check nothing I might have expected was going on down there. Is this for real? I pinched myself yet again. This time it really did hurt. This was definitely for real so why couldn't I believe it? We had been summoned by royal appointment, His Royal Highness, the right honorable Robert Fucking Plant to meet THE band. If the dog had bollocks then here they were. This was surely it!!

Led Zeppelin wanted to see us, no one else in the crowd, just us! (And I make no apologies for the excessive use of exclamation marks here!!!) This had to be one of the Twelve Dreams of Dr. Sardonicus. This was better than Bruce Willis sacrificing his life for the other people with big suits in Armageddon. Hell no, this was Armageddon!

After show afterglow

We went backstage, down some corridors that would have graced many a rock legend and into this tiny dressing room. It was very plain yet very regal (it had Led Zeppelin in it, damn it!) with two fifteen year olds, namely us hanging out with real rock stars. Why were we the chosen ones, I kept asking myself? Here we were and here they were and so totally relaxed, chatting away and in no hurry to get rid of us.

All the time we were hanging around backstage it never once occurred to us that we'd missed the last train home. I've no idea how we got home that night. Obviously we did. It's that precious moment when time just stops. Everything becomes etched so vividly in your mind. You're transported back and it's almost as unbelievable now as it was back then. *My Life on Mars*. We knew some of our friends were at the concert but they never had any of this. The weekend needed to end—and quickly. I had to get back to school. I WAS THE MAN!

Rock routes

Come Monday I made my way to school but decided I wasn't going to take the bus, I'd walk. Fortunately it didn't rain, hail, snow, no earthquakes, tornadoes so I was blessed. I took my signed Led Zeppelin poster with me and thought if I timed the walk to perfection, I would pass most of my friends at the bus stop. Let me think, seven bus stops to school. What time would I need to leave home and at which bus stop would I be worshipped the most? The one outside the bike shop—that was it! I won't be a second late. I fluffed up my hair dragging it over my collar, pulled my shirt out over my trousers and left my house. What a big daft grin I had that morning. I felt like I was backstage, waiting to go out in front of an adoring crowd.

The girl's school was only up the road and there were bound to be some *chicks* around (new rock talk). They loved Zeppelin, especially Plant and by now he was my best mate. Now what should I wear? I had to remind myself the satin pants wouldn't work. I carefully rolled up the poster so that all you could see was the black lettering on orange background and the words *Led*. Nobody spells *Led* like that except LED ZEPPELIN. I purposefully strode to school that day with all eyes following me. Utter bliss! Let them adore me like the 'rock star for a day' that I was. That night, rightfully, I should have claimed my prize. Damn, I was walking babe candy!

The poster child

All was not lost. We gathered at our usual haunt, The Griddle and Grill in the village with all the cool chrome fittings. It was like a 50s American
diner but with no America and toasted teacakes instead of burgers. They did have a James Dean poster as I remember and I'm sure in my dreams I saw Buddy Holly in there. Tonight was no dream, just me, my poster and together with the adoring mass—my new fan club.

I always believed in the music we did and
that's why it was uncompromising.
—Jimmy Page

We sat in our usual corner by the window but this time it was different. I sent Spud to the jukebox with instructions to 'slam in the coins and make sure it's only *Zeppelin*. Everyone gathered as I held court. Nobody let me pay for the jukebox selection or the hot chocolate that day. This is what it must be like being Jimmy Page or Robert Plant. I needed to get home and learn to play bass properly. This was for me. I was back to being a rock star. Later on, I claimed my prize when I got to walk the gorgeous Penny home. All the guys wanted to but today she was my reward. I was king for a day and she, my queen. I had the poster and she was slowly falling in love with me. Tonight I was the poster child.

Bittersweet

We never married but had four children Robert, Jimmy, John Paul and Bonzo until eventually we separated citing musical differences. I had the poster, she didn't. I was granted full custody of the poster and she ended up with a photo of her next to my prize Fender bass. The one I couldn't play *because I was crap*. As common law fans and without a pre-nup, I told her she should consider herself lucky, very lucky.

We kept in touch for a while but she became bitter. By the time Zeppelin had released four albums, I had never been to see her with the poster and she was particularly upset that each time they played I took someone else to the show. I don't miss her. We had what we had but now it's gone. I think I may have become a little over possessive but I make no apologies. I had my moment and if others had to suffer then so be it. The poster remained and was regularly available for viewing on the third Tuesday of every month at *The Zeppelin Shrine*, my bedroom. See, I wasn't that evil.

The following week I was back gazing out of the window. It made me realize years later what meeting my heroes meant and fortunately I never lost sight of that. If ever there was a chance to give someone a free ticket, a signed photo of someone they idolized, then I would always try to oblige. I remember the happiness it brought me and if it made their heroes real then it was worth it. It took me back to being that fan on that day. To be on the outside yet close enough to touch, was an extra special moment I will never forget. It made my dream real, if just for that day.

Great stories are timeless, I love reciting them. That whole chapter took me right back to the moment—and what a moment! I don't ever want to lose the excitement that only comes with memory. I don't think anyone should. Whenever times seem hard it's good to sit back and smile at the things that brought you pleasure. Miserable people don't do that. They want you to think that they've been dealt crap and their life sucks. It doesn't. They lack imagination. They lack the imagination to even want to look back. Why remember how to be happy when you're happy being miserable? Moments in time, bring you moments the next time.

CHAPTER 3

SCHOOL CAME AND WENT

BUT WHAT NOW

This train is bound for glory.

—Woody Guthrie

School came and went and I wasn't ready for work, not yet anyway. I had no trade and changing oil was about the sum total of my auto mechanic skills. Although I was good at parallel parking, valet parking hadn't really taken off in Britain and besides I wasn't keen on the jackets. My hair was too long and I wasn't prepared to put it in a bun under a stupid hat. Anyway this wasn't Sunset Boulevard or most of my time would have been spent jumping over puddles and being polite to awful women dripping in gold. My options were rapidly diminishing so I was left with a course in business studies. I could learn all about business and then run my own business—but what business? I tossed it around and promptly threw out a few other career suggestions. Maybe I could open a guitar shop, a rock memorabilia palace, a hotel for rock stars, anything rock star. They're all businesses but me running them? Suddenly I had a vague idea that I wanted to be a lawyer so business education started to make sense. Three months later it made no sense at all.

No direction home

I enrolled at a further education college in Didsbury in south Manchester. Further education in England was for people who had left school and had no clue what they wanted to do, so it seemed ideal for me. It was also on the bus route so that kind of swung it. Now I'd better find a course to pass the time. Nursing, I'm not sure I'm cut out for that and anyway I didn't like the idea of being turned down. Business studies it was. With fourteen girls and five guys in the class, it felt right.

Socially aware

I became a social secretary in charge of booking bands. This was more like it. The student ratio was seventy-percent girls to thirty-percent boys so I tried to spend as much time as possible walking up and down corridors, observing. It was also quite easy for girls to fall in love with me as I had all the tickets to all the shows. Before long, college had come and gone, though what I learned I'm not sure. It's where I met my first love Marie, who I later married. Not entirely true, she married me too. Still, she had the best record collection of any girl I ever met. Great times and two priceless heirs we named Jess and Joe, the only endorsement I ever need to know I'd done something right in my life. My heroes, I want to be them when I grow up! The two years at college brought with it some fond memories and some very questionable characters. By day, great fun and by night the students were engaged in another type of fun, although I'm not sure it was the police's idea of fun. They did keep a little room in their house free for them for frequent visits though.

If I were a carpenter—but I wasn't

Now I needed a job and pronto, but what? My carpentry, plumbing and electrician skills had ruled out any chance of a 'trade' and my options were dwindling. So I spent my time working in a take out burger bar, 'The Charcoal

Hob' but had no lofty ambition about being the Burger King, my torso was too slinky. This was no ordinary burger bar. It was the Rolls Royce of burger bars, the crème de la burg. Maybe I could work my way up, branch out and build a burger empire. I might franchise them all over the world and create a burger heaven for me to rule over. It wasn't on my original list and apart from that I had no clue where to begin. Tempting maybe but what about gigs? I'd be working nights and wouldn't be able to see any bands.

Hair today

Burger world was good for a while though and I did get to meet a bunch of vaguely interesting people. After a while I would try to tap them up for jobs but they all seemed to have proper jobs and I still wasn't feeling the slightest bit proper. I had to tie my hair back which made me feel like a rock star but it also made me look fairly unemployable to most. I made my decision. The job could wait, the hair needed to stay.

Later on someone else made the decision for me. The clientele were good, late night party chicks would come in, giggle and ask for free food. Occasionally if they flirted enough I'd oblige. It felt like headlining The Fillmore East with food instead of guitars. The chicks were my meat groupies. Time to get real. Where in the real world was I going to lay my hat. How was I going to earn my living? It was time for me to make some decisions or at least give the decision making process some thought.

What the hell am I going to do with my life? What's out there that is going to excite me? The head was going nowhere. I was in brain meltdown. I thought about it long and hard and even though I had some friends who were going off to university they were only idling their time away, they didn't really have a clue either. More schooling? I'd done enough and it didn't seem necessary if I wasn't entering the commercial world. I was comforted knowing we were all equally clueless.

No particular place to go

I never thought about a job in the music business, after all it's not something the career officer at school had much knowledge on. Still, I was left content that as a fan, I would take my place. I was sure I'd find something I liked.

I got a job and it was crap. It was so bad I can't even remember applying for it. Maybe I didn't get it at all. Maybe my mum got it for me and she just sent me along. How can you not remember how you got your first ever job? Maybe I was kidnapped and sold as a slave to work for pennies. I'll have to ask my mother. She had talked of giving me away as a child when I'd been bad. I don't think I could've ever been that bad to have ended up with this job.

A waste of energy is a waste of time

Whatever happened and however it happened, I was working as a filing clerk somewhere. I know it was in Manchester and it had five floors because my lasting memory is the smell from the elevator. I wish I could tell you what I did there. I've no clue but they did give me a pen. It was hardly the least bit inspiring and after being there a year I thought I was turning into them. That wasn't what I'd ever had in mind but it provided me with an income to indulge in my pastime, buying records and going to gigs. I was drifting aimlessly, but not for long.

Safe from harm

I got along fine with my parents and there seemed to be enough room at the house so I stayed there. I think it was okay although I never did ask. In hindsight, it probably wasn't a good thing as I wasn't paying any rent. My meals were cooked and my washing done so I wasn't really 'challenged.' I'm not ashamed. It was just the way it was and if my mother ever wanted to watch something on the TV I was usually fine with that. I was very happy at home and the money I earned was always enough for my needs.

After work, I'd be out the door before the fat bloke sitting next to me had fastened the top button up on his pants. He'd been there seven years and I was struggling being there just seven weeks. Nothing inspired me, not the people nor the place. I wanted out, but where? The one thing I did learn was to be content and do something just because it paid the rent. But that was not enough. I needed more. I needed something I would WANT to be good at. I would get the train home, change my clothes and hitch-hike down to Marie's where we'd sit in the front room and listen to albums all evening. She had *Hunky Dory* by David Bowie so it was love at first track. By eleven pm it was time to hitch back, whatever the weather. Then to bed, up again and the same old crap. Only one day nearer the weekend. One evening on my way home from work I picked up the Manchester Evening News to read on the train. I'd had more than enough time to stare out of the window during the day so I didn't need any more sight-seeing on the ride home. By now I wanted the train driver's job, anything than go back to work in an office.

The Evening News was a large provincial paper with a substantial readership and as Manchester always was a cultural haven for music, I'd grab a copy and check out the bands they were writing about. As it was usually pissing down with rain it also helped prevent random, inane conversations with nerds about the weather, that great British pastime. One morning on the way to work I gave up my seat to a pretty girl and she smiled. It was the best day I'd had in a long time.

Drifting aimlessly

As I flicked through the pages for some reason I stopped at the classified section, something I normally would never have done. I saw an advertisement for a salesperson at a record label called *Transatlantic*. I didn't know anything about them, in fact I'd never even heard of them. But all evening I kept thinking about it. I stared out of the window again and missed my stop.

I went to bed still thinking. This was starting to get dangerous. An eight hour work day hadn't provided as much stimulus. I needed to get bedtime out of the way and plan my exit strategy. The following day dragged even longer than usual until my lunch hour arrived. I took a trip down to the HMV store in the city centre. I searched through the endless alphabetical and specialized sections only to discover that Transatlantic was a folk and jazz label. Damn, not exactly my favorite genre. Old men with big cheeks playing trumpets, bearded ones with smaller cheeks who had their index finger stuck in their ear while yodeling and complaining. Where did rock and roll fit in all of this?

While you see a chance, take it

When I got home I applied for the job thinking nothing ventured, nothing gained. I didn't have a job in the music business so if I didn't get the job—then I still didn't have a job in the music business! Music had always been my life. Work was only a means to earn some disposable income to dispose of buying records. Now I was beginning to wonder, what if? I sent my application off to the record label and thought nothing more of it. I couldn't! If I had I would have spent every day gazing out of the window just dreaming about working in the music business. I waited and waited and then a few weeks later I got the standard letter back, *Thank you for your inquiry. We will keep your letter at hand,* which basically meant tough luck, you haven't got the job.

Secretly I hoped but in reality it's only what I expected. I thought nothing more of it and went back to my already bad job which now felt even worse. The place was worse, the people were worse and even the bathrooms looked worse. Six months later a second letter arrived, it was postmarked 'London'.

What the hell was this? I didn't know anyone in London so who was I getting a letter from? It was from Transatlantic Records, the same label that turned me down. I just kept looking at it and staring at the address, *Wardour Street, London.* Wow, to me it was like getting an invite to The Queen's Garden Party or maybe a round of golf with The Pope! Maybe it was from one of my mum's friends inviting me down to a Tupperware party or I'd be chosen to pull out the winning raffle ticket at Harrods and they would pay my train fare. Maybe it was a trial for Chelsea or Fulham. Maybe, just maybe I was talking bollocks. I looked at the letter one final time and was about to throw it away but something made me decide to open it. It was signed, Ray Cooper, Field Sales manager and it was asking me if I would be prepared to attend an interview. My God he wasn't a bastard after all. I hesitated and then read it again. They had kept my letter at hand. They really did want to see me! There is a God and his name is Ray Cooper and he wants to see ME.

Extra, extra, read all about it

Headline news.... 'Boy stares out of window but this time it's different.' 'Excited adolescent seen jumping on cars in sleepy suburb.' 'Sheep refusing to graze.' This was starting to feel weird, but good weird. I was starting to dream up all the possibilities in my head but I couldn't afford to get carried away. I would have been devastated. It was only an interview and I still might not get it. Stay calm Tone, stay calm. Bollocks, what's there to stay calm about? We're talking my life here!

I called Transatlantic and asked to speak to this Ray Cooper character. A girl with a London accent answered and put me through to him. He answered. It was him. He really did exist! He sounded really nice and very talkative and I was a mess, but an excited mess. Fortunately for me he still agreed to meet and said he'd come up to Manchester and we could meet there. What a relief! I had no idea how to get to London and if I did I'd probably get lost when I got there.

Mighty impressed

I put the phone down and the window beckoned. By now, most of the week had been spent looking out of it. This time it was different. 'Field Sales Manager' for Transatlantic Records, sounded impressive even for a label I'd never heard of. I hadn't met him but by now I was starting to fall in love. I went back to the letter he'd sent and smiled at it. I think it smiled back. I looked at his business card which he'd attached to it. Pretty impressive I'd only seen one business card before and it said 'Dave Wilson, Loft insulation. Estimates free.

WHOA!!!!! I just realized he said he'd come to Manchester but he didn't say when. He better not be lying. I called him back to find out and he told me next Wednesday. Couldn't he come tomorrow, later tonight? What was I going to do, it was Friday and if I had to wait all this time I'd go mad. Options nil, I agreed and planned what to do to pass the time away. I wonder if they do five day sleeping tablets. I wanted to be a hobbit and hide. It seemed like an eternity but Ray Cooper was coming to Manchester to see me. It was definite. I arranged to meet him outside the HMV shop on Market Street in the center of Manchester. My date with destiny was determined, 12:00 noon on a rainy Tuesday morning in August, 1974. Should I call Manchester United and tell them I'd changed my mind?

I don't want to wait in vain

I got there early and waited in anticipation. I was all excited when this bright yellow Volkswagen Beetle came careening round the corner with this Dumbledore look-alike at the wheel, jam jar specs and screwed up nose pressed hard against the windscreen peering through the driving rain. He had mentioned he would be in a yellow Beetle and it was around noon. There couldn't be too many yellow Beetles, could they? Dead cert, it had to be him.

I ran out from the doorway where I'd been sheltered from the pouring rain, waved out an arm and whoosh he'd gone, driving straight past me. 'Whoa!' This happened three more times until drenched and sodden I eventually managed to flag him down. He flung open the passenger door and screamed 'get in man'. It felt more like a kidnapping than an interview. Gandalf had picked me up and I'd been whisked away to meet a bigger magic man—a magic man who might give me a job.

Ray day

For a minute I thought this was fate. I'd stepped into the wrong car and I'd missed him. How would I explain that one away? And now a wizard was abducting me and I may never work in the music business. *Announce yourself magician—who are you?* Before I could say it, the magician smiled and said *Hi man I'm Ray, shit day.* Like I needed reminding. I was pissed wet through and feeling like a drowned rat. I avoided the obvious, *Did you not fucking see me waving my hand?* I shook my head and just smiled. I was wet but I was happy wet. I was here and wet or no wet I was going somewhere.

It got better. *Let's go to this bar I know,* he said. I knew it too and couldn't believe he'd even suggested it. So there I was on a wet Tuesday in Manchester being interviewed for my first job in the music business surrounded by topless, less than beautiful barmaids and picking at a stale cheese sandwich. Ray took a gulp of ale, burped, spat a bit of cheese sandwich across the table and sputtered, *Fancy the gig then, man?* I paused. I'd only ever had one job (the bad one.) Was this the selection process for the music business?

By now I wanted to hug him. It seemed inappropriate as we'd only just met. I'm glad I didn't. I'd have been like the drunken fool on a night out, *I love you, man. Thank you so much. You don't know what this means to me. I won't let you down. I promise. I promise I won't.*

The hostess was grotesque

Can I get you anything else, love? pouted Miss Coalmine 1948. I politely declined terrified what the 'dish of the day' might offer. If it was lard I'd have gladly swam in it. By now I was getting nervous. After offering me 'the gig' Ray asked, *Do you smoke?* I was hardly prepared for that one. Just as he said this, an escaped psychopath walked past me and let off this enormous fart! He turned, looked at me and burped. It smelt worse than the fart. I canceled my order of steak and kidney pie in case it knew him. My face creased up as I winced at the horrendous smell our friend had left. My eyes were starting to water. Ray gave me that look. He clearly thought I was the culprit. Surely I still had the job, I couldn't have lost the deal on another man's fart?

Ray then started to tell me the story of the guy who they had originally recruited for the job. It sounded like The Brothers Grimm, only grimmer! He turned out to be a reject from the 60s, a real space cadet who'd been warned three times in nine weeks for being stoned, twice by the record company and once by the police! Now there was no going back, least of all to collect the van he had abandoned on the motorway after running out of gas. We'll call him Ken. Why, because that was his name.

Van the man

He had neglected to call the record company to explain the situation. Obviously for him it had proved too complex to call and say, *The van broke down.* He just walked away and left it there. The police, seeing the record company's phone number on the side, called and inquired why they hadn't reported it stolen. Dilemma! First, it hadn't been stolen and secondly, they'd no idea the dumb ass had abandoned it. Calamity Ken ended up leaving through totally unrelated circumstances. He fell off the side of a mountain while skiing. He couldn't have gone to work even if he remembered where he worked and who he worked for.

Ray offered me the job as 'Northern Sales Representative.' I couldn't believe it. I still can't believe it, one of the most exciting days of my life. This was it, my big opportunity and I was determined to make it a success. I wasn't going back to any dead end job, no way. I went home and celebrated. Marie stuck *Hunky Dory* on the record deck and we sang to The Bewlay Brothers. The neighbors complained, like we cared? They clearly had no idea I was from the music business.

Transatlantic was one hell of an initiation into the music business. It's where all the lunatics assembled, convinced they could earn a crust. Talk about one flying over the cuckoo's nest, we had a whole flock! Miraculously, we did earn a living though, at least I did. Some of them never bothered to get up until noon and called the shops they should have visited to ask them if they needed anymore records. They just phoned the order in to the head office! I think one guy probably worked six hours a week, less if he'd been out a few nights on the piss.

Ray was a great boss. He saw a lot of himself in the rest of us. He was one of the lads who gave as good as he got. We took the piss out of him and he took the piss out of us. I think as I take the Engine Room out on the road I'll bring along a few of the memos he used to send us either reprimanding us for being dickheads or encouraging us to sell more records. I'm glad I kept them!

CHAPTER 4

ISLAND DAZE

Without music, life would be a mistake.

—Friedrich Nietzshe

I was offered thirty pounds a week, which was more than I was getting at the time so I wasn't going to complain. What the hell! I'd have paid them! I was given a van with a list of stores I'd be expected to call on. I had never driven a van in my life, except when I went to the Bickershaw Pop Festival and discovered that not every driving tip was in the Highway Code.

Slam van, thank you man

I was on the motorway doing sixty-five miles per hour, when I decided to drop down a gear. The Highway Code said that if you needed to gain acceleration then drop down a gear. Sounded easy enough. I don't recall any mention of traveling at any particular speed, so I casually slipped down a gear. All of a sudden about a dozen or so bewildered festival goers who had been seated peacefully in the rear came careening forward and into the front of the van. I humbly apologized, blaming insufficient information.

I hadn't even visited most of the cities on the journey plan I'd been given so I had no clue if they were north, south, east or west. I just assumed they were all in England. I hadn't told Ray any of this, and I sure as hell wasn't telling him now, especially since I had only just passed my driving test. After the previous employee hadn't turned out that well I didn't want anyone getting nervous, least of all him.

The ingredient of fun is the recipe for life

I started the job in August 1974 and the very first week there was a sales meeting at a hotel in Staffordshire, a little bonding and an informal way for me to be introduced to the team. I mustn't be late, I thought so I set off at six am to make sure I would definitely be there for the start of the meeting (which began at ten o'clock). Even though it was only a forty-five minute drive I wanted to be well prepared. It was my first meeting. Strangely enough I arrived early. I had a stroll round the grounds before stepping into this lovely English hotel, glorious in all its splendor. *Very nice!*

I stopped, looked round and noticed a moose's head on the wall. Wow, did they really have moose in this part of Staffordshire? I remember one in *Fawlty Towers* but that was further south and more moose friendly.

A warm glow of contentment

I sighed and still grinning, gazed around the place. I was here and nobody was sending me back there. Where? There, to a proper job. Finally I had arrived. I had made it into the music business. The receptionist looked at me and smiled and I smiled back. Now I really did feel like I was in the music biz. Two hours later and still smiling I was introduced to the sales team, mad as hatters, the lot of them. It was ten am and I'm sure four of them were stoned, two arrived late and three were a no show. Apparently this was reasonably good by their standards.

Baptism of fire

My first sales meeting wasn't really a sales meeting at all, more like a get together with old friends. When it ended and it was time to go I was summoned to be formally introduced to the hierarchy of Transatlantic Records. What a day, what a debut. What a pisser! I reversed my van, the one I'd been given three days earlier straight into the senior sales manager's car.

Ray's hiring skills weren't looking too good and my prospects, fairly grim. I climbed out of the cab and thought, *Well, maybe that was the shortest job in the music business. I'll be remembered only for my faux pas.* Not at all what I had in mind. *Nice one Ray. Where did you find this character?* said Alan who was Ray's boss. Thanks a lot for the sympathy; I felt bad enough anyway. It was the worst moment of my career and even before I had started my career.

Moments of magic

From the moment Ray met me at HMV that Monday morning I knew I was going to love this job. It isn't often you're given the chance to turn your hobby into your job. The window of opportunity had been thrown wide open. The dream was about to begin. Those early days at Transatlantic were magical and I'm just grateful the feeling never went away. Of course there were fraught moments along the way and times I thought the dream would end but we always found a way to make it work, a way to right anything that went wrong.

A good feeling to know

I worked with people who never took no for an answer and who helped whenever they could. They were persistent, daring opportunists, innovators and creative geniuses and the music industry was a better place with them around. We'll look at some of them later on in the book. They were my mentors and they were my friends. They are the ones who are there whenever and for whatever.

Raring to go

When I was selling records I would be up at the crack of dawn and at my first call when the store opened. I'd share a coffee with the staff, talk about whatever and laugh. Every day brought with it new laughter and fun and you'd have to remind yourself you were working. Different city, but always the same enthusiasm.

I'd call at the more specialized music stores selling my catalogue of mainly blues, jazz and folk. Like the staff at HMV, I would soon be familiar with what were the best selling titles and be able to use that knowledge to sell to new accounts.

The record business was starting to feel like home. I did really well in my time at Transatlantic and was consistently first or second in the top salesman category so it motivated me to keep working as hard as I could. I had some excellent stores and found the managers and staff very receptive. Everyone who worked in the record stores were avid music fans so we shared a lot in common. Business was good for everyone. People were buying music and I was enjoying selling it.

Moving on

After two years at Transatlantic, I moved to ABC Records where my area was extended and I started to sell their US catalogue to large UK retail outlets. It was hard leaving Transatlantic and Ray but I didn't have to wait long. He ended up at

ABC as sales manager! It was okay but Transatlantic was more fun. When they closed the operation down after just over a year I was ready for a move anyway. It was time for a new challenge so I started to put out some feelers. Little did I know what was ahead. I was about to begin the journey of a lifetime.

One happy family

Those of us working in the north of England were mostly based in Manchester and we'd meet up regularly, swap records, have some lunch and generally enthuse about what we were up to. It didn't matter if we worked in sales, promotion or marketing; we all knew each other and were enjoying life. Luckily I didn't have to think hard about a job and future prospects as others were already doing the thinking. I had a good friend, Terri, who was in charge of putting up displays for Island Records. She'd work the same area as me taking over entire store windows and adorning them with the coolest Island artwork. They were the coolest stores with the coolest displays from the coolest label.

No man is an Island

I loved all the music at Island and Terrie would give me posters which took pride and place in my home, so naturally I made it my duty to bump into her whenever I could! We were sharing a coffee when she told me about her housemate Bill who'd had a little altercation with the law. The prospects (for him) were not looking good. He had landed himself a CUI (collapsing under influence). He was driving his lady friend back to the nursing home one night and was a little worse for wear. Worse still, he turned into the parking garage and was followed by a police car. He pulled up, turned off his lights and yanked up the handbrake so the car was as motionless as him—and silently prayed.

One door closes

The officer pulled up behind, turned off his engine and slowly walked over to the car. He gently eased opened the driver's door and Bill, barely conscious, fell out on top of a flower bed. Island Record's thought it might be a good idea to search for a replacement rather than wait for the pending course case, the outcome of which I think we all knew the predestined conclusion.

Just the job

Terri was very persistent, *You have to go for the Island job, it's perfect for you.* I'm not sure why but I was at first a little hesitant. Did I want to make the move from sales to promotion? Maybe I was starting to think that suddenly all the great relationships I had built up in the retail sector would now mean nothing. I would have to start all over again. I must have been mad. Island offered me an opportunity that no one else ever would. Why would I even consider hesitating?

Persistent people with good intent

Terri wouldn't let go and for that I'm eternally grateful. She called Bill's boss and arranged for me to go down and meet him; now the more I thought about it the more I was warming to the idea. After all, I'd been looking for a new challenge so why not? Anyway it was Island Records and it was the best job in the world!

As I took the train to London to meet with Phil Lowery, the Head of Promotion, I started to get really fired up. I wanted this job and I wanted it badly. After making the transition from sales to promotion, I was very confident this new challenge was the perfect fit for me.

Island of dreams

This was the most exciting label on earth. I'd grown up listening to their artists and now I might have an opportunity to join their illustrious ranks. This was too good to be true. I had always adored this label from the moment I discovered music. *Free* and *Traffic* were two of the first records I ever bought and since then I had started to collect their entire catalogue, so why was I hesitant when Terri suggested I go down for the interview? It was starting to bug me but it no longer mattered. I was here. The train journey from Manchester to London Euston was almost three hours but it felt more like ten. I'd started to drift into 'What if' territory. What if they do offer me the job, how cool would that be? You haven't got the job yet so don't build up your expectations and risk being disappointed, I kept reminding myself. They have said they want to see me though, so just maybe.

My Island home

I arrived on time, no delays and by now I was relaxed and ready for my meeting (did I mention it was at Island Records). I got up, gathered my belongings and climbed off. A shrug of the shoulders and a big sigh told me 'This is it.' I shuffled down the platform at 'London speed.' (Why do you always walk five miles an hour faster when you are in the capital?) I stepped on the escalator that would take me down to the depths of the underground tube station. I looked for the green one, The District line and my destination, Stamford Brook.

My musical birthplace

I ambled along the streets to the famous St. Peter's Square, the home of my all time favorite record label, Island. I walked up past the park admiring the beautiful houses (and women) and there before me on my right, was Number 22, my spiritual home—the home of *Island Records*. The most beautiful building I'd ever seen.

I started to think of all the great records that had come out of this building and how they helped shape my life, and now I was to meet some of their creators. I walked up the steps to the reception desk.

It looked like something from a Roxy Music video with two gorgeous models and a backdrop of brilliant artwork. Some of the posters I had already seen in the back of Terri's car. Here they looked even better.

Phil Lowery please, I purposely announced myself. *Is he expecting you?* I was immediately offended. Of course he was expecting me. You might be gorgeous woman but don't you dare send me home!

Yes! I smiled and was directed down some steps to the 'War room,' the famous room where all the employees sat around a huge table with a giant white board running the full length of the wall telling you what was happening with every act at any moment in time. No matter where anyone was seated, they could swivel around on their chair and find out who was doing what and where. What a totally brilliant, cool idea.

Closed for business

The place looked amazing and I wanted to steal everything off the walls. It was totally different from Transatlantic where Ray had worked in a tiny office upstairs at the warehouse. The only thing I ever wanted to steal from there was the receptionist. Funny, the place was empty. Not one solitary person was in the room. Where the hell are they? I'd arranged to be there at two pm and the place was empty. They had better not gone out of business? This better be the dream I was looking for. I didn't have to wait long.

After ten minutes the door flung open and in strode an entire football team! These, I was later to learn were my future employees and they'd all been out playing football during their lunch hour. The score was 2-2 and the final result would be decided on penalties. That explains the delay.

Meet and greet complete

Out-stretched a muddy paw and Dave Domleo, the center forward, extended his greeting. Dave was General Manager and was smiling inanely. He'd scored the match winning penalty. Two steps behind strode John 'Knocker' Knowles, christened such as a result of a lethal left hook. Bringing up the rear, Phil, dirty knees, bearded and grinning, *Tony, great man, give me two minutes. I need a slash.* A relieved Phil sat me down in his corner and asked me when I could start. My second interview in the music business was as bizarre as the first. I'd already landed the job and this was just a 'meet the lads' get together. I only wish I'd arrived an hour earlier, I might have played in the game!

Moving in

The whole vibe of the place was fantastic; the people were brilliant and I was raring to go. I can't remember the exact day I agreed to start. Who cares!—I was about to begin working for Island Records, the label I'd adored as a kid. And they were going to pay me as well.

When I first started in the music business back in the 70s record companies proudly boasted they had 'record people' who worked there. I will forever be grateful that I had the opportunity to work for two labels that were run by three such men, Jerry Moss and Herb Alpert (the initials which made up A and M), Chris Blackwell the man who started Island and the big daddy of the family who had just agreed to adopt me.

The family that plays together

Island was my first adventure into the world of promotion and what an amazing place for an initiation. It's where I learned my trade. It was the place where the artists grew up with the people who worked there. It really was a family. Between 1978 and 1988 I worked at Island on three separate occasions. Even when I set up my own promotion company they still retained my services but independently. They allowed me to work with other artists as well as their own. I can't think of another label other than Island who would have done that. It was like waving your kid off to university but telling him he could still live at home.

A great place at a great time

Island Records will remain, much like Atlantic Records, an institution in the music business. Great things happen at great places in great periods of time. The fifty years Island Records has donated, from my own personal viewpoint, is unlikely to ever be surpassed. How could it?

Cos these are the days of our lives
They've flown in the swiftness of time
These days are all gone now but some things remain
When I look and I find no change

—Queen Days of our lives

It's a business so vastly different today that it would be impossible to be able to support a band the way they did with U2. The money they poured into them in tour support knowing as much as they did that it would just take time. Time they were happy to give them.

The reward time gave them was returned when Island was experiencing financial difficulties and couldn't pay U2 their royalties. They knew how important the label had been in allowing them room to develop so they happily sat back and waited. They weren't sticking any knives in just to get a paycheck. The days our lives indeed.

Thank you for the days—The Kinks

It is what it is and what it always will be, a truly great record label that attracted some truly great people both personally, professionally and artistically. They stuck with their staff like they stuck with their artists. Everyone had fun while providing so much. I'm sure I wasn't alone thinking of the times you spent away from work, still talking about work, if you can call it work.

I often wonder where life might have taken me if I hadn't learned what I learned from working there at the time. Too many legends from that Engine Room to mention, yet enough to savor the memories. What an amazing time to work with bands and share what you have learned.

From the inside looking in

The music business seems like an alien outpost, a place that doesn't really exist. I've seen some remarkable achievements from some equally remarkable people.

I've watched mountains grow out of molehills and I've seen people squander that one chance to change it all.

Most of the people in this book were unheard of when they took their risks and when they made their mistakes. They had the courage and the belief, in themselves and in one another. They kept their dreams alive. They really did think they could pull it off.

CHAPTER 5

OPPORTUNITY

THE SLINGS AND ARROWS OF OUTRAGEOUS FORTUNE

I am just a dreamer and you are just a dream.

—Neil Young

In this chapter, we will look at some of the people I worked with, how they approached opportunities and what they did to capitalize on them. We'll look at how to prepare for opportunities and how you can create your own. We'll also see where you can identify them for others.

Grasp opportunity by the beard as it is bald behind

A Bulgarian proverb telling us to act on opportunity, take the initiative (although I'm not quite sure about the Bulgarian with the bald behind grasping his beard). You've probably heard the phrase 'nothing ventured, nothing gained.' Very true! If you don't reach out and grasp the opportunity you might never know what could happen.

No regrets

'Opportunity comes but once,' but personally I don't believe that. I think we are faced with many opportunities in our lifetime. I admit I've squandered a few both personal and professional, who hasn't? No point in pondering over 'what if' I much prefer 'what's next.' To look back is futile, look forward to the next and make sure you are prepared for when it happens. Was it your fault, did you let an opportunity pass you by? Could you have done anything differently?

Treat every opportunity as if it's the last one you'll ever have

Once you've identified an opportunity, if it doesn't go the way you planned remember it's still an opportunity. If it's not the right opportunity for you then see if there is someone you know who can benefit from it and allow them the opportunity. It may happen that they do the same for you sometime.

My first big opportunity came with that ad in the local paper for the sales job at Transatlantic Records. Some incompetent had placed the ad in the wrong paper. It was in the *Manchester Evening News* when it should have been in the trade publication *Music Week*. It proved very favorable. I got the interview and the job, and then a thirty-year career! My hobby had become my job. I went from selling records out of the back of a van for sixty-dollars a week to running my own promotion company in the UK and working with some of the world's leading artists—some whose records I'd bought as a kid!

Don't squander the chance

Opportunities don't just happen because of luck. You always need to be on the look out; be ready and prepared for whenever one might arise. When I spotted mine there wasn't any point in pontificating over it. Go for it, I told myself. I didn't have a job in the music business so what did I have to lose? While you may get more than one opportunity, you might not, so treat every one like it's your last. The opportunity was there, now it was up to me, it was a chance to turn my life around and get a job I could never have dreamt of. For me, it was a golden opportunity.

The realms of possibility were saying, what if I did get the job, then what could be next for me? Then years later, when I had the opportunity to move from sales to promotions, I jumped at it. Why wouldn't I? After the first opportunity allowed me to enter the music business and gave me the chance to establish myself, I had all the confidence I needed to go and pursue this one. It opened up doors for me and once I was in, nobody was shutting them.

Vision without action is a daydream—action without vision is a nightmare

That's a very old Japanese proverb. If you don't have the vision you won't spot the opportunities, and if you are not looking for them they'll pass you by. The most successful entrepreneurs in the music business have been able to spot every opportunity. It's here, both Simon Fuller, creator of American Idol and manager of The Spice Girls and Simon Cowell excel. And I had the good fortune to work with both of them.

Midas man

When I first met Simon Cowell he'd already tasted failure. He was in his 30s, been bankrupt twice and was living with his parents. The experience proved invaluable. He never looked back. I don't think you'll meet many people with as much drive and determination as Simon. We didn't always agree. I was a radio man and believed you needed radio to make hits, quite selfishly because it kept me in a job! Simon knew he could do it with or without radio because he signed artists that meant something on TV and was convinced he could sell to the public via that route. He was one-hundred percent right, in fact, we were both right. I told him they wouldn't get radio and they didn't! They weren't exactly your average releases, one was The Power Rangers and the other WWF (World Wrestling Federation).

Between them they went on to sell a million and a half copies and although it proved no threat to Elvis or The Beatles and left their legacies intact, it did pave the way for puppets and wrestlers to make records. During the years I worked with him one half of BMG (Arista Records) was no longer prepared to support him so he moved to the other (RCA) and to instant success with the same two records that Arista had just passed on!

You can wonder about taking opportunities—or you can be wise and take them

All Simon's record sales were generated from the TV exposure they got. He was arguably the first executive in the UK to see the power of television in selling records. Labels previously advertised albums on TV but had concentrated on radio airplay for hits. Simon saw it differently and proved the point with his next signing, a couple of actors from guess what, a TV show. These guys had never made a record but Simon was convinced this was an incredible opportunity. Motivated by a relentless determination, he was a man on a mission. He was going to deliver and big time.

A golden opportunity

He was given the heads up from a girl in sales, Denise, who told him about the street buzz being generated by these guys called Robson and Jerome. They were starring in a very successful BBC television show that was broadcast on a Saturday night and proving especially popular with the ladies! They had sung a rendition of the Righteous Brothers' *Unchained Melody* the previous Saturday and the TV station's switchboard had been bombarded with calls, creating an unprecedented demand in the stores. And all for a record no one had even thought of releasing? No one except Simon Cowell.

Simon seized the opportunity before any record company was even aware of the demand. He called the TV show and asked the producer to tell the actors that he wanted to sign them, and record the song immediately. They were already very successful actors and turned him down several times, saying they just weren't interested in making a record now or at any time in the future. In his book, *I don't mean to be rude but....* he claimed to have phoned them three times a day for seven months. Knowing Simon I can believe that! Apparently one of them had threatened to take legal action because he was harassing him so much!

Eventually, they relented. Simon offered them $100,000 each saying they could keep the money and if they didn't like the record he wouldn't release it. How's that for confidence? It was Simon's first ever number one. Robson and Jerome's debut album went on to become the best selling record of 1995. Their follow up was the best selling album in 1996 and Simon Cowell was on his way to many more number ones.

Not so lucky

They were offered three-million EACH to make one final album. They politely declined and after becoming millionaires returned to acting. They had become BMG's most successful act. Simon Cowell created an opportunity that not only benefited himself but the artist, the record label, all the staff and me! Well almost, the record didn't benefit from too much airplay (remember I told him they would never make it on radio). He decided not to use me for the follow up but instead employed another independent promoter. Even after a number one record it ended up with less airplay than the first. I was right after all.

Mr. Opportunity

Simon Fuller's career has propelled him into the top ten most influential media people in the world (*Time Magazine*). At age twenty-five he signed Madonna to a publishing deal with her first single *Holiday*. Two years later he found an artist named Paul Hardcastle with a record based on Vietnam, entitled '*19*'. It shot straight to number one. From these humble beginnings, the successful '19 Entertainment' empire was born. He now runs a variety of companies including management, TV and publishing. Simon Fuller is as successful as any of the acts he manages who include The Spice Girls, Annie Lennox and American Idols Kelly Clarkson, Carrie Underwood, David Cook and others.

Perfect timing

His timing and ability to seize opportunities are unparalleled in the music industry today. The brains behind American Idol, he has turned it into the most successful American TV show in history.

It's a stroke of pure genius. The audience vote for their favorite artist, they then release the record by the act they have already voted for and it's an instant hit! Brilliant idea, how could it fail? They already voted for them so why wouldn't they make it a hit.

Simon Fuller helped change the way Americans watch television. And to think the concept for Pop Idol which he originally launched in the UK was turned down by every major TV network before Fox picked it up. Along came Cowell and the dynamic duo were born. Batman had found his Robin. And in case you didn't know, Batman went on to become one of television's top celebrities.

Fight like a brave, don't be afraid.
No one can tell you, you got to be a brave.
—Matchbox Twenty

Creating Opportunities

The best type of opportunity is where you help to create it. When Matchbox Twenty first came to the UK they were unknown even though they'd sold three-million albums in America. Due to the demand from other territories we'd been given very little time to put together a regional radio tour doing interviews, local press and the like. I met them in Scotland while the rest of the band did additional promotion in the south. By splitting up the band we doubled up on the amount of promotion. The following week we were on sixty-two of the most important radio stations with the end result a Top 40 single.

Help create your own success

Even though these guys were big stars in America they were still prepared to do the necessary ground work. They didn't need to but their manager Michael Lippman, a veteran with a wealth of experience in breaking acts internationally was very keen to break the UK and saw this as the perfect opportunity. Success in the UK acts as a gateway to Europe and can be vital in breaking an act abroad.

Consequently, we were able to cover most of the important regional radio stations in a very short space of time. The industrious Matchbox Twenty helped create their own success.

You can wonder about taking opportunities—or you can be wise and take them

Opportunity in the right hands is optimism, in the wrong hands pessimism. There may be an opportunity for a promotion at work, a chance to further your career but it just might be the wrong time. It isn't about grabbing every opportunity, just identifying the right one and remaining optimistic and positive.

Finding opportunities might mean finding them for others just like when my friend Terri found me the Island job. She had already identified it wasn't for her, either by choice or by timing but that it would be ideal for me. Being granted that opportunity allowed me a new direction, to work with new people and accept new challenges.

Once I accepted the job, it then gave me the opportunity to set myself up as an independent promoter. I was able to keep the old job but also accept the new one I was offered. The final outcome was that it became three opportunities in one, Terri's, mine and the record company's. All of this was the result of somebody identifying an opportunity even though it wasn't for them.

If you believe it enough you won't need to convince others

In 1980 I was working with U2. They released three singles together with their debut album *Boy* and my job was to take them to radio stations to talk with whoever would have them. All the while I was hoping the hard work would pay off and opportunities would come our way. November that year was incredible. There were a few of us at Island Records who believed in the band and were convinced they could be huge. Rob and Neil in the press department had done an unbelievable job getting journalists along to see them play and were starting to get some really good feedback.

At the crossroads

All their efforts culminated in a prestigious *New Musical Express* front cover at the start of the year. Up until then there had been no significant breakthrough at national radio or television and we knew we'd struggle to survive on press alone. In order to maintain great press coverage, the media would need to see others pick up on the band.

To get radio and television interested you needed the press. It was a catch-22. We were at the crossroads and needed a break otherwise it would have been impossible to keep the momentum going. Out of the blue I received some amazing news.

It's good news week

Tony Hale, a network radio producer and a contact of mine loved the band. He enquired if they were available to record a session. WERE THEY AVAILABLE—damn right they were available! Around the same time I got confirmation that Granada TV's network show *Get It Together* wanted to book them. I couldn't believe my luck. All my Christmas's had come at once. I say luck but in all honesty I had been working hard on the band for most of the year. We all had and felt we deserved this break.

Be patient, the greatest achievements can take the most time

This was the most significant result we'd had from national radio and TV in the UK. Now others were really starting to believe in them and we were starting to think, just maybe? These were hugely important programs with ratings to think about and I was immensely proud that a major TV station like Granada thought they were good enough. I knew U2 had always been waiting for this opportunity and how much they deserved it. It was a pleasure giving them the good news.

The people who get on in this world are the people who get up and look for the circumstances they want, and, if they can't find, make them.
—George Bernard Shaw

Finding Opportunities

I was totally committed to this band. I thought they were brilliant, great guys with a great manager. We had become good friends. I believed in them and in return I had their trust and confidence. They knew I was the right man for the job. We'd grown up together learning our trades as we went along, they on one side of the promotional fence, me on the other. Every opportunity we had we'd be out there meeting new people in the media and making both friends and fans. At the same time I was building strong relationships with the media, especially Granada TV where I always felt welcome.

Sharing Opportunities

Every opportunity any artist was given was my opportunity too. Their chance was my chance and I would be judged on my ability to deliver who they wanted, when they wanted. If they wanted a big name I would do my utmost to get them and in return they were always receptive to the newer acts, the ones who needed the breaks. Working with new artists, I was able to tell them about the times U2 struggled for recognition, just waiting for that one opportunity to come and always looking out for it. Although we all played a part, their greatest achievements were their own doing. If you spot an opportunity and it isn't right for you maybe you know someone else who can benefit.

I also saw some that I was able to identify better than the artist. It would be too cruel to mention names because this fellow learned the hard way. He declined to do a TV show that I thought was perfect for him because he didn't fancy it. It was a perfect show for him yet he couldn't see it. The worse thing of all was that it wasn't one of those tacky shows where you can understand the reasoning. Later on, I found out that the reason he declined was that he had asked the presenter out one time and she turned him down. Touché!

Pride coming before a fall? One hell of a fall! Seemed more like inflated male ego to me and it pissed me off because I had to make excuses as to why he wasn't available, when he was just plain stupid! Worst still, he didn't feel it was his fault, he was adamant it was hers. It was my first experience of a solo artist splitting up. He slowly slipped away into nowhere land.

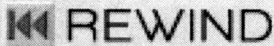 **REWIND**

OPPORTUNITY

1. **C**ircumstance: Opportunities happen when you least expect them. Be prepared.

2. **H**unger: If you are not on the look out there are always others hungry for the opportunity.

3. **A**nticipation: The adrenalin rush for what the opportunity could bring.

4. **N**ow: Nothing ventured, nothing gained. If you don't try you'll never know.

5. **C**reate: Make an opportunity that will give you a better chance of success.

6. **E**ndeavor: Accept a chance to change, not just your career but your life.

7. **S**ustainment: Maintain the desire to keep looking for opportunities.

CHAPTER 6

RISK

THE THRILL OF THE CHASE

Dancing on the edge is the only place to be.

—Trisha Brown

The music industry is a risk business, it always has been. I can't think of anyone who got anywhere by just being lucky. They all took risks and for some it became a way of life. Everyday you're competing with someone for something and if you're not taking a risk then the people around you probably are. They might be releasing a single, is it the right one? They could be booking a tour, will anyone show up? The marketing department might be planning an ad campaign, wondering if they're reaching the right demographic.

If you're unknown you'll try anything to get yourself known, and if you're well-known you're always looking over your shoulder for someone who's trying to knock you down.

You can risk releasing a record too soon or leave it too late, either way you risk failure. If your record label doesn't think it's good enough they won't risk releasing it at all. Everything that involves the relationship of the artist with those around them will be closely connected by one common denominator, *RISK*.

Reach for the moon—if you fall short you'll still be among the stars

If you're an artist and you're not innovative and creative you can be over before you've begun. You *HAVE* to be prepared to take those risks. In this chapter we'll concentrate on the risks that some of the artists I worked with took. Risks that were so big, had they not taken the initiative, there would have been no second chance. Without taking a risk, they really could have lost everything. So what is risk and what can we learn from it? You probably don't realize it but we take more risks in our lifetime than we would care to imagine. As a nineteen-year-old going for a job in the music industry, I was taking a huge risk. What did I know about working in the music industry?—let alone what it entailed. Being a fan and buying records or going to concerts was one thing but having a job in the music business was something entirely different. I think I must have been mad!

Better to want something bad than to expect something good

It never put me off, it just made me think of all the possibilities and how much better I could make my life. While I dreamt of the possibilities, I also prepared myself for the stark reality that maybe I wouldn't get the job. That way the disappointment would be easier to take. Who was I trying to kid? Wanting the job so bad made me confident that something good would come from it. Evaluate the implication before you take the risk. I said to myself, *Give it a go, what have you got to lose?* I didn't have a job in the music business so if I don't get it I still wouldn't have a job in the music business. Technically I did have a job but it wasn't giving me any personal satisfaction and I was certainly prepared to risk any security there for an exciting new challenge. What was I risking after all, making myself happy?

There's no point being apprehensive and wondering if something negative could happen, that indecision could prove fatal. Nothing is ever a dead cert and there are never any guarantees. Whatever you do might end in disaster but if you don't take those risks you'll never open your mind to what might be. Be positive. Believe you are making the right decision and do everything you can to ensure you get the right result.

There's a risk attached to almost everything you do. Some are scared to risk ending a relationship, but why? They won't get married in case it doesn't work out. If it's come to an end then end it! They don't want to risk being lonely but they're prepared to risk being unhappy. Where's the logic in that? You can't win. Do you want to feel you failed in your relationship or would you be happier knowing you had failed to be happy?

Why take a risk if you don't believe you can succeed

I won't eat this in case I don't like it. I won't buy these clothes because I might put weight on. I won't go to this place on holiday or drive this car. WHAT THE HELL!!!! Don't get up in the morning then, because if you feel like that the whole day might not go the way you planned. But if you stay in bed all day there's a risk the roof might fall in or the house might burn down. Then what? You might be taking a bigger risk than you think just by not talking a chance on something. Never blind yourself to the possibilities of what might happen. Try to imagine risk as excitement instead of fear; push out a little and then you just might want to push out a little more. Taking risks can become a little addictive too, like the poker player who risks his hand. He may be bluffing. If he wins he'll do it again and maybe when the stakes are higher. If you approach risk like you are going to succeed then you're likely to be the better risk taker.

If there's a chance then it's a chance worth taking

It might seem ludicrous to some but to a risk taker they've worked it out in their head and they're prepared to give it a go. Go on, take a risk. It may not solve all of your problems but it'll piss enough people off to be worth it! Some feel it's the fear of failure rather than the anticipation of success. Of course nobody plans to fail but if they do they need to know how to deal with it. Put it down to experience and learn from it. Better still, pull it off and experience the utter jubilation when all the hard work has paid off and risk has turned to opportunity.

To gain which is worth having it may be
necessary to lose everything else.
—Bernadette Devlin

If you are in a band every day you are out there hoping others will believe in you. Every little thing you do will be judged, by a record company, by a journalist, by an audience. If you're in a band you must be prepared to risk everything. Just signing alone is a huge risk. A record company will invest tens of thousands into an act and risk losing it all if they don't sell. A group will get dropped by the label if they underachieve. It's a performance based business. You are only as good as your last record. If you're having hits and making people money then you're okay but the moment you don't—you're out! The major record companies have begun to shy from risk. The mavericks of old, the music men have gone and accountants and lawyers are running the business. It's down to the independents now to throw caution to the wind and take those risks. It's all about getting a return, but didn't a return on an investment always require you to take a risk? There were never any guarantees. You'd cash in but if you took a few risks the return on one could make it all worthwhile.

Belief is the endorsement we have in ourselves and in each other

The most successful groups of all time are making it because of the risks they took and it's been the same for over fifty years. All through rock and roll and right up until the last decade, the music industry was all about taking risks. Where would Elvis have been if he hadn't gyrated his hips? It might have seemed a pretty risky thing to do back in the 50s but for rock and roll it was a defining moment. What about Madonna, our Lady Risqué? Throughout her career she went out to shock and even though some periods were received better than others it never stopped her desire to want to take more risks. If an artist isn't prepared to take a risk then they shouldn't have gone into the music business in the first place. If the artist isn't prepared to take risks it's hard to get a manager, because a good manager would always want to be trying new things.

The willingness to fail is the preparation to win

U2 is a band known for taking risks right from the beginning. They knew they were in a highly competitive business and that they needed to stand out from the rest. They had the confidence and belief in themselves that all bands need and they had the support of a label that allowed them to indulge in their dream, to be the biggest rock band in the world. They could have moved forward at a steady pace, slowly building a career but they always liked to push their boundaries, presenting themselves with new and different challenges. It's what makes a good band great, the difference between safety and daring. What has helped them retain their enormous fan base has been that desire to try different things. They attract a new generation of fans while retaining the old ones and it's been that way ever since they began. U2's phenomenal success has been their willingness to try things and by their own admission, not always successfully.

Many times we are wrong—but sometimes you only need to be right once

Bono had always been one for taking risks, especially when they played live. Right from the early 80s he would get lost in the moment when he was on stage and try some pretty scary stuff. He would climb the speaker cabinets at the side of the stage and sing from the top of the columns. He'd see the balcony and look for a way to climb up on it. If there wasn't a way to get there then he'd find one. Each time, their tour manager would carefully follow him trailing the microphone lead behind to ensure it didn't wrap around anything and pull him down. One slip and he'd have been rock history.

Satisfaction lies in the effort not the attainment.
Full effort is full victory.
—Mahatma Gandhi

It was all a part of the U2 show and something their old fans had gotten used to. As the fans grew there was always a new audience for Bono to enthrall with his favorite pastime and still the same band and crew to scare the shit out of! Then, along came Live Aid, when everyone saw that magical moment brought about from one Irishman's little walkabout. He didn't do much climbing that day but he still wandered over speaker cabinets and security people to get to where he was going. I doubt Bono knew what he was going to do that day until he got on stage and pulled that girl from the crowd. Making history is never planned.

This was one risk that turned into an incredible opportunity. It might have stemmed from a previous risk they took a couple of years earlier which proved to be the first big turning point for the band. In 1983, they arranged to play a natural amphitheatre in the Colorado Mountains, the now legendary *Redrocks*.

The inevitable conclusion is rarely the original plan

What happened on that day was nothing anyone could have planned, expected and least of all dreamed. But it was these two events that went on to become as significant as anything that happened to U2 before or after. The band had been scheduled to play on June 5th and had been assured that weather conditions around that time of year would be favorable.

As a result of the strong relationship the band had with a TV producer named Malcolm Gerrie, who had launched a very influential music show in the UK called The Tube, U2's manager Paul invited him and his crew out to Denver and asked them to record the show. U2 paid for the crew and their travel and all they wanted in return was for the show to be shown on Channel 4, the TV station that broadcast The Tube. Malcolm agreed to show some of the film but said the network would never allow him to show it all. The band just left him to it, safe in the knowledge that he would do everything he could for them but with no guarantees. The band had sunk all their money in to this. It had to work and if it failed there was no money to fund anything else. Effectively U2 would be over. They paid for the filming, gave Channel 4 an exclusive but retained ownership. Good move. But only because U2 were resilient to the end with that unfaltering believe that this would work, it would be a risk worth taking.

Just before show time the rain came down, and continued to come down. They were praying for it to stop because by then had everything had been paid for and cancellation of the film crew and rearranging the show just wasn't possible. The only thing that had to happen was the show. Without a show they had no film and everyone stood to lose everything. Barry Fey the promoter was adamant they should pull the show. He was prepared to issue everyone a full refund in the event of safety because by now the electricity was arcing between the speakers. This was shaping up to be a disaster of epidemic proportions. If the arcing was to strike a band member there could be a fatality.

The show must go on

Only after Dennis the tour manager gave the go ahead would they confirm the show could go on. The band made an announcement on the radio. If it was canceled they offered to play the following night for free. They even stood there in the rain to meet the crowd on their way into the amphitheatre and personally thanked them for coming. Five thousand people turned up that memorable night. Although the place was only half full the setting and the course of events that followed became the backdrop for arguably the greatest rock film ever.

Divine intervention

Miracles can happen, and did. Somehow the heavens were literally looking down on them. The rained stopped and what was left was the most incredible setting and something that no amount of filters or set design could ever have created. U2 had lit beacons above the rocks on the side of the stage and the flames were shooting into the sky and giving off the effect of a battlefield. It added an almost ethereal feel to the whole thing. Through the flames there was a fine drizzle and due to the altitude and it being cold, the steam was actually rising off Bono! No one could believe what they were witnessing. The show itself was nothing short of magnificent but what they saw from the resulting footage was even better. Back in the mid 80s, MTV was a hugely powerful promotional tool in helping break bands. U2's courtship with America was about to pay dividends. Big ones!

True to his word Malcolm Gerrie had managed to persuade MTV to screen the film in its entirety. As if this wasn't enough, MTV'S sister company *Showtime* had a huge fan who just happened to be the guy running the company. He was totally impressed and agreed to show the entire film. This was one risk that turned into one hell of an opportunity.

This chapter shows the monumental risks that helped elevate U2 to become one of the worlds most successful bands…. ever.

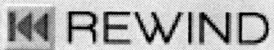 REWIND

RISK

1. Determination: No risk is worth taking without the determination to succeed.

2. Assessment: Part of the process of risk management, seeing where the dangers lie.

3. Resilience: Your ability to stick with it and do all you can to succeed.

4. Evaluation: Look at the implications of taking a risk. Both positive and negative aspects. Will it affect others? Could it lead to job losses?

CHAPTER 7

COMMUNICATION

GROUND CONTROL TO MAJOR TOM

You may be disappointed if you fail, but you are
doomed if you don't try.
—Beverly Sills

Let's look at how you communicate and how to work with the different type of people you will encounter not just in the workplace but in everyday life too. Some people are a pleasure to do business with, others a necessity and you will need to adapt to whatever situation you find yourself in. Today's world requires we spend more hours with work colleagues than with our partners. It's a relationship and you have to treat it as such. You have to work at it. All it requires is a little give and take and a little understanding of others.

Communication is an art form, it's priceless

The music business is a communications business, always has been, always will be but where in business or in life would you not be expected to communicate with someone? I admit I was lucky to have a job I loved but irrespective of what you do, how you approach your work is vital to how you well you do it. Your attitude to work reflects your attitude to life and someone who is happy in their work is usually happy outside of it too. If you can't be bothered and are intent on being an asshole then skip this chapter, piss off a few more people and come back for your fifteen minutes of fame in the next chapter.

Come up and see me, make me smile

Being charming never did anyone any harm. Approach your job with enthusiasm and optimism and you'll find the people around you will be just as keen to make it a happy environment. Smile. Be nice. It isn't that hard to do. It's integral to the art of communicating and essential to the way we do business. Even if you don't particularly like your job, make the most of it. Keeping positive and smiling through present circumstance helps you look forward to moving on to a better working environment. Laugh. It's infectious. No one likes to have to look at a miserable face around the work place. If you're miserable then you'll make those around you miserable too. Why should you expect others to be tolerant of your attitude or mood swings? Going to work vibrant and ready for what the day might bring makes you popular to have around. Having energy and vitality leads to a motivated work place with motivated people. If you like to be liked, be likeable!

Personable people take particular pride

Basic people skills are something you should have learned at home, please—thank you—get out of the fucking way. Possibly your parents didn't like you or maybe you didn't listen. Being respectful, trustworthy and honest you'd think would be taught at childhood but that's not always the case.

The one thing that never changes through generations is good manners. Make sure you have them and if you don't have them, GET THEM! Myself, I was always fascinated by the human race. I met a few that hovered around it but mostly my experiences were favorable. It's the people I met along the way that steered me in the direction I went both personally and professionally. It enabled me to identify the people I wanted in my life and taught me how to work with others. Make those choices whether as an employer or employee. You will find your job becomes more satisfying rather than something you're obliged to do.

The art of YOU

Impressions count, especially first ones and for a lot of people their lasting memory is the first time they met you. If you change, they remember how you were not how you've become. If you're obnoxious the first time the chances are they'll think you can be obnoxious again! Be remembered for the right reasons. Firstly though you have to WANT to communicate? It's how you get to know people and it is how they get to know you. Make yourself available. Put yourself in situations where you will meet people and then see how you are with them. Was it a pleasant experience? What was it you didn't like? Did you feel relaxed, confident? Did it feel right? Did it scare the crap out of you? Did you feel like a fish out of water? If it was good, then that's good and if it was bad it doesn't always have to be bad. Nevertheless bad is bad—fix it.

Identify your weaknesses

Your skill at communicating will ultimately be left for others to decide but no matter how good you may think you are there is always room for improvement. As you begin to integrate and meet more and more people, your communication skills will develop and you'll find yourself better equipped to adapt to situations. There will be different obstacles and it will be for you to work out how best to deal with them. You may also find some who are jealous of your ability to communicate and feel threatened by your popularity. They feel resentful and may want to attack you (not literally!) or intimidate you, while others might try to belittle you. These are all things you will be able to deal with once you have perfected your interpersonal skills. What may once have seemed like a problem will be nothing more than an irritant. Your ability to deal with the many different types of characters you will encounter is of benefit to all.

There is always something you can do better

What do you feel are your strengths and more importantly, your weaknesses?
Do you find it difficult meeting new people for the first time?
Are you more relaxed when in the company of colleagues?
Are you comfortable in one to one situations?
Do you wait until you are spoken to?

What do you want to get out of your job. If it's money, then would you do any job for money? If that's the case then don't complain if you hate your job, you chose it! Would you rather use e-mail than interact face to face with people? Which of the above do you feel the most uncomfortable with? Once you've asked yourself the questions then start to work on where you feel the need to improve.

Confidence grows where conversation flows

It isn't always necessary for you to start the conversation. The other person might be more assertive and confident and could help relax you simply through their outgoing personality. Listen to what they have to say. If they are good communicators there will be some body language. If they smile when they speak to you, you'll probably find you will too. Conversation will come naturally and you will feel more at ease. If you're at some sort of social gathering where people are in abundance, look for someone in the room you would like to get to know. Approach them and introduce yourself. If they take a dislike to you, don't outstay your welcome. You can't have it every way and if someone doesn't take a shine to you the first time around, sticking around won't change anything. The next time could be totally different. They might hate you even more!

It's all in a smile

Smile. That's smile, not smirk, grin, gloat or slobber, all of which are deemed predatory. A smile is warm and pleasant and invariably generates a reaction—a smile back. They may be happy for the introduction and begin a conversation. You may find others similarly attracted, interested in getting to know you, who will also be keen to introduce themselves. First hurdle over, you're allowing yourself to relax in the company of others, you want to be a good conversationalist and you're interested in what the other person has to say. Feeling happier and more confident? Good start! You are getting to be popular.

Good company makes for good conversation

On the other hand if you struggle with the quieter, less outgoing personalities then you'll need to try a different approach. Not everybody is going to respond the way you hope they will so you'll need to play another hand. Being shy is one thing, being dull, something entirely different. When did you ever hear of a quiet person pissing someone off? Shyness can actually be quite attractive and there are those who carry it off very well. While they appear a little quieter and more reserved there's also an allure. Sly shy!

Shy for a while

And then there are the sometimes shy, the ones who aren't shy all the time. In the right company they become much more confident and self assured, until some idiot ruins it by saying, *I always thought you were shy?* Then they retreat back into their shell. If you're shy, try to be around the type of people who help you feel more confident and relaxed and less conscious of your weakness.

Shyness is never a weakness

Depending on what type of career you want it may be a hindrance. If you lack assertiveness or self confidence and you're required to sell a product you may not be suitable for that particular job. It's not a problem, there's a job out there for you, just not that one. Go and find it.

The telling truth

Honesty was, is and will forever be the best policy. People have respect for you if you're honest about circumstances and situations, whatever they may be. You can't be the purveyor of good news all the time but you can be the bringer of the truth even if for some, the truth hurts. When I promoted records I would never hide the truth. I was paid to tell clients what the media thought of their records. If they thought they were bad, I'd say so. Some pretend all is well when clearly it isn't. Why report back that a record is being well received when it isn't? What's the point? If it was well received then they'd play it and if it wasn't then clearly they wouldn't. This isn't rocket science. It's not as though people wouldn't find out the truth anyway and if they didn't like a record then why the hell was that my fault? I didn't record it, I only promoted it and I was being paid for my ability to get it to people not bend their arm to play it. It's never worth risking your reputation by lying. You'll be found out and from then on people will doubt you. Tell it like it is or don't tell it at all. If you're on the receiving end, never be frightened by the truth.

Truth as reality

Telling the truth is far more interesting, except sometimes for the artist! If they are out promoting and doing interviews then they have to accept that they need to answer the questions they are asked and not the ones they want to answer! A few years back, a friend of mine was scheduled to interview a famous cricketer who had recently released his book to the public. He had been successful for both club and country and now that success had provided a wonderful opportunity to release his autobiography. Unfortunately for him, on the day of the interview news broke of an illicit affair—his obviously—and it was in all the morning papers. He walked into the radio station and the very first thing he said, before even offering a Good Morning was, *I'm not saying anything about....*

Arrogance as ignorance

Everyone was flabbergasted. How arrogant! Did he really expect it to be ignored when it was already front page news? The audience would have expected him to be asked the question and while my friend would have not labored the point, it still needed addressing. Much to his dismay and horror he was sent packing without the chance to say anything, least of all promote his book. It could have been an apology or, *I'd rather not discuss it,* but to come in with such an arrogant attitude and announce I'm telling you what you can and can't talk to me about is deplorable.

Take that look off your text

There is a whole new way of communicating now and it's called the Internet. So many people find out about so much online that you have to be able to reach out in cyberspace to a new generation. I'm fine with that but I see it as an addition and not as a replacement to the methods of old. What happened to wanting to communicate with people? Why would you pass up seeing the look on someone's face when you bring them some good (or bad) news? Today dating is done via text messaging or e-mail and they'll dump you in much the same way. You know when someone doesn't love you anymore because they hit the delete button on their address book! Disposable has come to be the nature of everything we do from trainers, to music, to relationships. The general sentiment is, it'll do for the moment then I'll just drop it and move on.

Meet me at cyber dinner

I was horrified to read in my local paper about a tweeter party, a tweety or whatever. The gist of it was that a bunch of people had *known* each other for a few months but had never met? Maybe their emails had been intimate but now they suddenly thought it was time for a get together. Real human contact! It sent out alarm bells so I read on. I thought meeting in person was what you WANTED to do once you'd struck up a relationship over the web? Don't you want to socially interact and lead up to physical interaction? Don't you want to speak to someone when you are looking at them—preferably at the same time? This illustrious bunch did finally *meet* and wasn't it the part you're glad you missed. The picture in the paper was nothing short of ridiculous. There were nine people seated at a dinner table, two were hammering away on laptops while the other seven were staring, tweeting and sending texts on their cell phones.

Not one person was looking at the other let alone speaking to them but the funniest thing of all was that strategically placed between each was a glass of wine! To think that these people actually thought it was time they met, so they got together to do exactly the same as if they were in different continents. I'm thinking social malfunction here and an appalling misuse of technology. Remind me not to invite them to my next party.

I built my life on relationships and I'm very glad I had the chance to do that. Give me all the technology in the world and I still wouldn't change a thing. I'm especially glad that my children made the right choices too. While they love technology and grew up in the technological era it wasn't at the expense of what they enjoy the most, interacting personally with people, face to face. Friendships get established and people are there to help you when obstacles get in the way—when life becomes a bitch. Show me a machine with emotion that can help you when you're feeling down, can help lift your spirits or inspire you to take your career to the next level.

In these real life situations where you're interacting face to face, nothing can be hidden. You are literally exposed; anyone trying to hide anything can be easily detected. Many people, myself included, won't do business with people until they have met. Think of entrepreneurs like Richard Branson and the amount of business he has done on the golf course, how he spends time with people before he goes into business with them. He needs to get a feel for what they are about and needs to know he can trust them. For him and for many others, there is too much at stake.

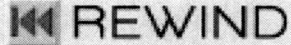 # REWIND

COMMUNICATION

1. Notification: Don't turn up expecting to meet someone unannounced, let them know. People have schedules. Respect them.

2. Embrace: New technological methods of communicating along with traditional ways.

3. Truth: Honesty and respect are basic human ingredients, use them to your advantage.

4. Willingness: Want to communicate. It's how you get to know people and how people get to know you.

5. Obnoxious: Over zealous behavior can make others avoid you. Showing off becomes tedious.

6. Ramification: First impressions count. A person's lasting impression is formed the first time they meet you. Behave badly and you'll live to regret it.

7. Karma: You get what you deserve. Personable people take particular pride.

CHAPTER 8

PUBLIC RELATIONS

THE GREATEST STORY EVER TOLD (YOU HOPE!)

The starting point for improvement is to recognize the need.
—Masaaki Imai Kaizen

Public Relations, where dreams are thought up and reality can get you in a lot of trouble. Over the years people have come up with the wildest ideas. Where there wasn't a story they'd invent one. Some are believable, others utterly unbelievable. It's the type of job where if you've got a vivid imagination it has to be worth a try. My line of business was promoting records to radio and television. If it wasn't for us then how would you get to hear about your favorite artists or buy their records? You owe me a beer!

Write about now

You would think PR is about relationships with the public but it's actually about relationships with the media as a way of getting to the public. Maybe they thought calling it MR instead of PR might be a little confusing. Just think if you were female and referred to as an MR (Mister) specialist—worse still if you specialized in MR! Would you really like to be applauded for your MR stunts or better still your MR methods?

If you believe in it enough you won't need to convince others

PR is about creating awareness and maximizing opportunities whatever business you're in. PR is about people believing in you. You're the messenger. It's you getting in front of the media trying to grab their attention. If you're an obnoxious irritable tapeworm, they won't listen to a word you say. Alternatively, if you're hawking a piece of crap around, you're wasting everyone's time. If it's true and believable then you're halfway there. It's easier to sound convincing if you don't have to make it up. If you keep inventing stories make sure they are the same ones. Once someone hears a different story to the one you've been telling, you'll be tagged a bullshitter. If that happens make sure you're a good one. Lose your credibility and it's gone—forever.

Whenever I was out there promoting a record, my integrity and my reputation were always at stake. I'd spent many years and a lot of time and energy nurturing these relationships. For me, there was no room for compromise. I could never look someone in the face and tell them something was happening with a record if it wasn't.

Personally I never thought it was worth ruining a relationship for the sake of one record. You're there to get your product noticed and can only do that with good people and good product! Believing in it yourself, can go a long way to have others start believing in it too.

Know who you are working with

Every artist is different. I would never work with an act without first meeting them. If they had made a great record but had very little to say then my job was to protect them—or more than likely protect them from themselves. When you were trying to promote a record to radio it always helped if someone had heard of the artist, if you'd had some good press. Then once you had press you needed to keep getting more press. And for the press to write about you, there needs to be a story, something interesting the public wants to know about. They're not there to make your bands famous or to help break the acts. They're there to sell papers.

When saying nothing works

Some bands can do no wrong in the eyes of the press. They create a mystique by saying nothing and when they do speak it's very brief, just a quote. It's a technique that worked very well for bands like The Stone Roses and New Order.

They genuinely thought the music spoke for itself and there was nothing they felt they needed to add. Journalists like to put words in their mouths. When Ian Brown the singer with The Stone Roses was asked if being from Manchester helped with their success he said *It's not where you're from, it's where you're at.* Very succinct and guaranteed to shut up any smart ass journo.

If anyone suggested New Order were awkward for not doing interviews they felt it wasn't even worth defending. If they wished to accuse them of being boring they'd agree! *We are boring,* they would say. It left journalists with nothing other than frustration. They (the journalists) feel that the artists need them and they'll do anything for publicity but that wasn't always the case. Not so long ago in the UK it was cool to be that way, especially if you were not consciously trying to be aloof or awkward.

Pressing issues

Traditional publications today are forced to compete with the online press, governed by less strict guidelines. They can go that little bit further by being a bit more controversial. They like a bit of smut because for some that's what sells. People like to read about celebrities being caught sniffing cocaine off strippers or seen leaving a house they shouldn't be at in the early hours. Circulation figures are plummeting at print media. Everyone's looking for a story and the more outrageous the better. If there isn't one they'll make one up but don't stretch the realms of belief too far or you'll get sued. Anything proved to be false and defamatory can give rise to a hefty law suit so be careful who you slag off, the tamest of targets can have a savage beast of a lawyer. They'll go straight for the jugular and anyone they bury is all the more money for them.

In some lawsuits the lawyer ends up with more publicity than the artist you were trying to lie about in the first place. Many publications when caught will print an apology. It's usually tucked away as a column on an inside page when the original story may have run as a lead item on the front page. Not much justice there. If you're the guilty party it may cost you millions nowadays and no one is prepared to take that risk unless their source is a one-hundred percent trustworthy. If it costs the paper, it could cost you. File under very costly mistake. The end result could mean no money, no job and pretty lousy prospects. You're done! Want some press then? Have as much sex with as many multiple friends, family, fans as you can, preferably all at the same time. Leave the wife and go off with her sister, her cousin, her brother, her dog. Anyone, just do it! Don't do it quietly. Everyone needs to know. There needs to be disruption, divorce, a feud of some sort. Sex sells and it always will, especially when someone more interesting is doing it.

Money matters

If they are intent on clearing someone out financially, better still. Don't bother with anyone who's already broke. There's no point, no one cares. Stay with them, at least that way there's a broke and penniless story. If they get lucky and get rich, you can still claim the credit. If it wasn't for you—there'd be no them!

Brotherly love

There have been some great press people over the years at record companies. You could almost *see* them thinking! They are always looking for an angle, something they can excite journalists with. For example, if there are brothers in a band it's always better if the brothers don't get along. No one wants to hear about brotherly love, they need sibling rivalry, famine, pestilence and war—and plenty of it. Nice brothers don't get press, they get invited to dinner parties. Horrible, rude, loathing brothers are popular with everyone other than with each other. They're press darlings and they always make good copy. People will buy them drinks hoping they'll get pissed and say something, possibly get laid. By who—who cares? Hopefully someone they've never met who is equally famous and/or drunk.

The thirst Noel

There was never any possibility of people not knowing when Oasis had a new album out. The press adored the Oasis boys from the very start primarily because Noel and Liam didn't adore each other! They would get pissed and fight. Strangely enough everything would be drearily calm until there was a new album out. They'd be out walking their offspring around leafy parks and sharing ice cream cones. Then all hell would break loose and they'd be at each other's throats. Noel would leave the band. *I never want to see that bastard again.* The press lapped it up every time. It's funny how he was always okay being in the band in between albums when they didn't need the press. Everyone knows it doesn't make good press to live in peace, the media mock you. You need to be a mess or at least do something! If they find out you're a decent human being they'll try to get you to act out of character. They'll turn up at some function you're at and start taunting you. They'll say something hoping it prompts a reaction. They want you to look disgusted and then as soon as you show some emotion they grab a picture. It isn't you but what they made you for that moment.

Tell it like it is

A promotion person needs to be accountable. If a manager wanted to know how things were progressing with their artist then it was my job to tell them. If you couldn't, then clearly you didn't have good relationships with the people you were dealing with and shouldn't be doing the job. People didn't play records on the radio because they liked me. They listened to them and told me what they thought of them because they respected me and knew I was expected to give other people that information. I was paid to report back to record companies, managers and their artists a true and accurate reflection of the progress being made on their record. Constructive reporting is vital in helping to plan the next move. If I was struggling I would say so. In my job that type of communication and feedback was everything. It still is. I was employed to get records on the radio and acts on television. While I could never guarantee that, what I could guarantee was that at any moment in time I had the answers for the people who needed them. If a record was not on the playlist then why wasn't it on. Would it go on?

Working with the best

Good managers aren't frightened by the truth. I built up a good relationship with Matchbox Twenty's manager, Michael Lippman. Here was a guy who'd seen it all, who worked with the best (and probably the worst) and he didn't suffer fools gladly. All he asked of me was honest feedback about his band. I was more than happy to oblige.

If it's worth doing then it's worth doing properly

Creative PR will collaborate with the acts and their manager to create stories. Again, they need to be convincing. They'll tell them to go to dinner with someone, where to go, what time to be there and they'll be sure to give some important journalist and their photographer a heads up. They'll conveniently be there waiting, thinking they have a scoop. They get a picture that could be worth a fortune and the act and their publicist will ensure it gets fed to the right papers. Everyone is there helping everyone else. Getting publicity, as long as people are making money, is fine with everyone! Publicity and having their photo taken is what the artist thrives on. It's a strange business when they spend half their life trying to get famous and have their picture in the paper, and when it happens and they are famous, then they spend the rest of their life going round with sunglasses on and a baseball hat trying to not get noticed!

Vary it up a little

Think of new ways to do things. Tried and tested formulas that were new and exciting at one time may seem tired and outdated today. The last thing a PR consultant needs is to be tagged passé.

It's important for a good PR agency to have strength in depth. Experience is vital, new blood essential. Balance the mix. Have young enthusiastic whippersnappers working with technology, finding new ways to get the message across. Compliment the team with older more experienced people who've survived on reputation. Make sure they understand one another and can work in unison. Where in the past a journalist might have jumped on a story because they liked the scam element, a new up-and-coming writer might not even glance at it. The PR consultants that succeed are the ones who stay one step ahead of the pack. It may have worked once but it might not work again. Once you think you have an *in* with someone, they might be out, especially today where traditional press is rapidly changing. If your friends get sacked, follow your foes. They might be the ones you need to befriend!

Drink, be merry and be—drunk

Journalists like to drink, it's a hobby. I would never imply that it's a job requisite and certainly there are those who teetotal but there are also those who teeter when totalled! LESSON: Try to see them at pre-pub opening times. Breakfast is good, if you're lucky they'll be nursing a hangover and more likely to listen than risk opening their mouth and hurling. Say what you have to say and leave, it's better for everyone.

Try to remember

Send them an e-mail. If they reply then the chances are they remember who you are, either that or they think they loaned you some money. If they don't, remind them who you are. If you partook in the festivities and can't remember who you are, make something up. Timing is of the essence. You need a reply and an acknowledgement so hit them (not literally, though tempting) when you think they are able to focus. Don't give them time to fall asleep. They'll return to the office, then there's that cushion of five or six minutes when they just focus on their laptop. Don't be the message they fall asleep to. If they're awake, the chances are with modern technology, hitting the reply button on the e-mail could very well prompt a one liner. RESULT: Move on. The rest of the day will get better.

Look at what you can achieve instead of what you might expect

Be realistic, if it seems improbable then it probably is. Find an achievable goal and try to reach it. See what you did to get there and see if you can take it to the next level. Setting your goals too high can seem like failure when in reality you may have done really well but set your targets too high. No point looking like you missed out when it's just bad planning and poor judgment. I believe in starting small. If you grow something from nothing, you can watch it flourish and share in the development. You can monitor the progress and inject the right ingredients at the right time, whether that's resource, manpower or money, whenever it is needed. The end result is all the more rewarding. It shows that a plan and strategy have been carefully thought out and that general awareness was the result of a gradual build. There is less suspicion of hype.

Get in front of people—it shows you are determined, confident and mean business

You need to, it's how things happen! I have yet to see a machine with passion and I've never been able to throw my arms around an e-mail. I embrace technology. I'm limited but I love to learn about new ways to do things.

When I start to get my head around it and it's gone, there's always something new. There is so much new media available to us since the explosion of the Internet, it would be physically impossible to get by without it. I met a journalist not long ago who actually said people don't seem to want to call him anymore. They'd rather e-mail a press releases, some tour dates, sometimes even random text. This was a guy who never used texting so he wouldn't have seen anything anyone sent him anyway! What I found worrying though, was the fact that they hadn't asked him how he wanted to be contacted and just presumed that he would prefer e-mails. There's a lesson here—presume nothing. All you need do is ask!

Is it up to standard or down to price

Just remember, NEVER be tempted by price. If someone is attracting you by the money they are offering don't be seduced by it. Suddenly someone is prepared to pay you more than you'd anticipated. What you think is a dream come true can be a nightmare waiting to happen. If they think they can tempt you with the offer you need to be sure they can provide their part of the deal, that being the back up. If someone thought I was a good record promoter and they needed me they might dangle the cash carrot. Don't be fooled into thinking it's because you're good. It can mean they're useless and they NEED you. If they can't deliver and the back up you are getting is non existent they'll blame you. If it didn't go according to plan they'll deflect the blame on you and not want to pay you. Suddenly it isn't looking as tempting.

The whole music business in the United States is based on numbers, on unit sales and not on quality. It's not based on beauty, it's based on hype and it's based on cocaine. It's based on giving presents of large packages of dollars to play records on the air.

—Frank Zappa

If you put a price on something then you are saying this is what I think it is worth

If in doubt and you want the job but are not one-hundred percent convinced about the people, walk away. If you can't, maybe times are hard and the offer is too good, then make sure you get it in writing. Insist on getting fifty-percent up front, that way at least your time and efforts will be paid for. The reality is you may never see them again and it'll cost you twice the price to chase half the fee.

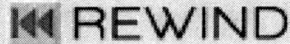 REWIND

PUBLIC RELATIONS

1. Teamwork: We all need to work together so be understanding of what others want.

2. Enema: The ability to know how far you can go before you become a pain-in-the-ass.

3. Assertiveness: Get your message across in a clear understandable manner.

4. Maximization: The role of PR is to get the word out and maximize awareness.

5. Whacky: Publicity stunts can still work if they're original.

6. Outrage: The press lap it up but remember it has to be true. If they find out you're a bullshitter, it will backfire.

7. Report: They are paying you to promote them, whether the news is good or bad. If it isn't happening, tell them.

8. Knowledge: Know what you are talking about and use that knowledge well.

CHAPTER 9

MOTIVATION

FIRING ON ALL CYLINDERS

There's nothing you can do that can't be done.
—The Beatles

I have been motivated for as long as I can remember. When I was a kid playing soccer I would always want to improve my skills. I had professional role models but I also had teammates I looked up to. It wasn't envy or jealousy, but respect and admiration. If they had a part of their game that they were better at than me it would make me want to improve. If I watched these players closely and I saw how they got better at their game then I knew I could too. I realized our team was so good not just because of our ability but because we were all motivated by each other.

In the pursuit for perfection

I admired other sportspeople too when I was a kid and I don't think that boyhood memory ever changed. It motivated me and made me want to be a winner. I wasn't sure at what, probably back then a footballer, but it left an impression that if you try hard you can achieve things in this life. If you set the perimeters and the goals and strive to get there, then it's your race to win.

Going nowhere fast

Back in my first job, I didn't feel like a winner. I couldn't see myself being there long so I never courted a promotion. Although I was pleasant with people, I wasn't that bothered about befriending them. We had little in common and once I moved on, I knew we'd go our separate ways. My lack of motivation gave me a *couldn't care less* approach, about almost everything to do with the job.

That lack of motivation taught me how important it is to have a job you like. I needed a reason to get up in the morning and this wasn't it. If neither the people nor the place inspired or motivated me, I'd have to go. So I did.

Work occupied so much of my waking hours and I had to have something that satisfied me. I knew what I wanted but didn't know where to get it. From the moment I joined the music business the first person I ever met, Ray Cooper, motivated me and he still does. He knows me too well. He knows what I am capable of and if he saw me being complacent he'd give me a kick in the butt. Motivation! It's the buzzword nowadays. In business, in training, in leadership and in speaking, it's everything everyone ever wants to know. Why they have it and why someone else doesn't. It's a little overplayed. It's become a business within a business. It's everywhere.

Motivation is the new *modernism*. We never had athletes decades ago that needed motivating, silent film stars or anyone. It's what they did, what they took pride in and they wanted to do well. Now we have a word for it. We call them motivated. A person will usually find the motivation if they want to. It's in their blood. And sometimes they'll need others to tell them.

Motivational or motivating

There's a HUGE difference between a motivational speaker and a motivating speaker. A motivating speaker is inspirational, you hang on to their every word and you believe them—they're sincere. You have faith in them and in what they are saying. And a motivational speaker does not. I don't need to be told the things that motivate me I just need to see them around me in everyday life. A good motivator will ask people to find out what it is that motivates them, then encourage them to work at it and bring it out of themselves. A bad one will tell them give me all your money and do this.

Let's get motivated

There are so many motivational speakers out there telling you to throw your arms in the air, introduce yourself to the person next to you, tell them your name, ask them how they are, shag them. Whatever they tell you to do, everyone is happy to oblige. I thought that was hypnotism. *Get motivated* tends to sound a little robotic. It's telling people how to be motivated but how can we do that when we are all different? Look at the type of things that motivate people rather than what you need to do to get motivated. Motivational speakers are fine, some of them. They are a form of life and others are a form of pond life. They have a job to do but they're not for me. I'll pick out people I meet, listen to what they have to say and draw my own conclusions. I'll be motivated by what I eat, drink and where I sleep. I love working with motivated people because they are very easy to get along with. They work hard and play hard. They are self-motivated at whatever they put their mind to. Productivity levels increase, you work better and deliver more when they're around. They are the right type to motivate others.

111

What gets us motivated

We all get motivated by different things and we all have to identify what it is that gets us motivated. For some, even getting out of bed is a problem. They think of any excuse not to get up, it's cold, it's raining, I don't feel well, there's nothing for me to do there. All this adds up to one thing, They don't enjoy their job. Anything rather than go to work and when they do get to work they are counter productive because of their lack of motivation. This lack of motivation rarely lasts and it won't take someone long to realize they are surplus to requirements. The motivation goes along with the person. They're sacked!

Look at yourself

So how can any one person get another motivated? Well they can't by telling them because we've defined why that doesn't work. The only way they can get anywhere is to show the other person how motivated they are and let them see the results for themselves. Maybe it's a pay raise or possibly a promotion. Maybe that other person is popular in the workplace and that might appeal to them. Quotes are a wonderful means of motivation. Prophetic statements stop and make you think. They let you apply your thoughts to their words. They help conjure up imagination and possibilities. They make you dream.

Wisdom begins in wonder.
—Socrates

Socrates motivates me by inspiring me. He makes me think about what I do before I do it. He plants the seed. As wisdom begins in wonder, wonder too what motivates you. Find it, identify it and use it. Everyone is motivated, not only by different things but in different ways. Once you find out what gets you motivated, it will help keep you motivated. Getting motivated is one thing, staying motivated is harder. The nature of human beings is to wander a little, they can lose focus and their attention wanes. Those who keep focused are able to do that because they are self-motivated. They want to succeed in what they do.

Cash not credibility

Be honest with yourself about what motivates you. If you say you are motivated by money then fine, people can understand that. But if you say you are motivated by *the creativity* and all of a sudden you're not getting rich from it and your motivation goes, you lied and you've left yourself wide open to criticism.

People who are motivated by money are usually always motivated by money. Their sole purpose in life is to get rich. They are capitalists through and through. They get up in the morning and want to make money. They want to make money right up until their head hits the pillow. Even as they lay there, they think about making more money.

Money, money, money

It's the only thing on their mind. All they are interested in is the financial return. If there was chance of being successful at something but it didn't make money they wouldn't be interested. Is it greed or is it being motivated by money? Is there's a difference? This kind of motivation doesn't inspire anyone apart from like-minded individuals. However, if that person has always been that way you can't really complain later if it starts to piss you off. They were always motivated by money and they still are. So where's the problem?

Motivated and alone

Where this person's motivation measures wealth in monetary terms, other motivated people are wealthy in life. They are usually achievers at work. They get promoted, earn bonuses and help inspire others. A motivated person can be motivated in several ways. If they are full of life and have a positive attitude they will feel good about most things. They will feel motivated by a relationship, with a partner, their parents. If they have done well at work and are happy with where they live that will keep them motivated. Life feels good.

Highly motivated

Top athletes are highly motivated. They are driven with the desire to win and by constantly keeping motivated they expect to succeed every time. If they lose it makes them all the more determined the next time. Another type of motivated person is good at removing obstacles. If they are undertaking a task where everything is stacked up against them they look for a solution and don't become despondent. They work their way through it by keeping motivated.

Motivation from energy

Creative energy flows when you are around motivated people. You find everyone contributes their own ideas and offers their own solutions. They look for ways for something to work rather than reasons for it not to.

Motivation and inspiration are different. Inspiration is often about the moment, it passes and then something else inspires you. With motivation, it can be a person or a project or almost anything. But it's usually constant. Never let circumstances quell your enthusiasm. A motivated workplace is infectious, you each motivate one another.

Then there are times you may feel a little less motivated but it's still there. Inspiration comes and goes. In the Olympics, Michael Phelps was an inspiration to everyone. He pushed himself to win every competition and to focus totally on the next race. His self-motivation and will to win is what inspired us. Once the Olympics were over, he was all but forgotten. He inspired us for the moment. Motivation is what drove he and his teammates to win every race. His colleagues saw him win and it made them want to be winners too. His determination to finish first made everyone who competed against him super focused, they too wanted to win! He motivated everyone around him and made them all feel like winners constantly.

A waste of energy is a waste of time

I found it a waste of energy if I had to spend time motivating others. If you employ the right people then they are self-motivated too and your time can be better spent elsewhere.

Motivated people rarely need supervision. With the right guidance and understanding of their role they can be trusted and left to work independently. Motivated people have a strong work ethic and a determination to succeed. They are ambitious people. If they are ever unsuccessful, be assured that at least they have tried their best. They are driven by the will to succeed rather than any financial gain. Money is rarely the single most important ingredient driving them. If it comes, it's the reward.

Rally around one another

In times of adversity this is imperative. If gloom stares you in the face, the end result can be grim if you don't have people around you who believe you can succeed. It always felt good to work with like-minded people. We were all out there to paint the bigger picture. The canvas was stretched out and one by one we'd add our part. It's a great feeling when everyone can share in each other's success.

The one thing that drives us all in wanting to accomplish anything in life is motivation, it even gets you out of bed. But if you don't want to get out of bed then you won't get out of bed, those types are a little more difficult to get motivated because they're in bed and asleep. Motivated levels can become a little suppressed when you want to smack them in the face. Get up or get out, of MY face. If I want to do something I don't have to think about doing it, I just set about doing it. With some people lack of motivation can be nothing more than a lack of self confidence. That's not a big deal in itself but it's something you can work to alleviate. It's where motivation may be lacking through a fear of failure, people feel apprehensive and worried that if they attempt something there is always the possibility that it won't work.

We're back to getting out of bed again and if you think that way then forget it. Every moment of every day something *may* go wrong but guess what, invariably it doesn't. You got through yesterday didn't you, and here we are today! The person who believes in themselves enough is the motivated person and it's they who can have an influence on the end

116

result. They approach everything they do with a different mindset. They are excited at the prospects and they want to tell others. That excitement becomes infectious! When their excitement transcends to others then you can really start to have some fun. Motivation levels increase, you're even more motivated. Settle down!

Over motivated, whoa boy

That's when you need to slow down a little because over motivated can be a little *get out of my face!* You become over everything when all you need to do is *get over* everything. While we know you're excited there becomes a limit to how much you talk about it to others. What can be enthusiastically shared within family members can be sometimes too much when it becomes an obsession and all you talk about is you. It's the difference between being over enthusiastic and over indulgent. Excitement people can handle, self obsession wears thin. Polish up on your interpersonal skills and be able to detect when you're going a little too far. They're peering down at their watches and you don't have one, they're looking for a reason for anything, except you.

Fine lines, from possibility to probability

It is a fine line however, when a passionate person with a belief in what they're doing still has a positive effect on those around them. If they can do it then you can do it. And if they've already done it once then they can do it again. A motivated person acts as a mentor. You see them as a role model. Anything that once seemed possible can look a little nearer to being probable. *It can, if YOU think it can.* Motivated people are dream makers, they see the happy ever after, they have the drive to put themselves out there. They have a love of life which generates initially from a love of what they do, but they still have a love for others. They don't want it on their own, they want to share it with others. They want to share in every part of the process and believe that whatever they achieve can act as an inspiration to others.

Back to me, and back to us

Enters TM! (Totally Motivated)—Tony Michaelides. It's why I wrote this book, it was an undeniable thirst for the adventure I had. I was given an opportunity and all I had to do was be motivated enough to accept the challenge. Was I motivated…. HELL YEAH, I WAS! I couldn't wait to get out of bed and propel myself in to taking my hobby to the next level. Why go out and work at something I didn't enjoy when someone was going to pay me to do something I loved. That was plenty motivation, my motivation was my way of showing my appreciation and it wasn't that difficult. I don't think I needed a masters degree for that and neither do I think I needed anyone standing in front of me explaining that you have to want it bad enough. I had it and that was good enough. We're born hungry, that's why we take to our mother's breast. It's our first chew of life, a taste of what's out there. (No guys, not women!) We need to STAY hungry though, we're all a bunch of lousy homo sapiens until we prove to ourselves that we can do it. And we can do it, maybe not all of it but we can do a lot more than we maybe think we can if we just put our minds to it. Desire does leave the bedroom you know.

Back to me. I'm amazing! I made the decision to do this then I brought a bunch of people in to help not because I had to but because I wanted to. Not only did I want to, I couldn't wait to. It wasn't to bathe in the glory or see my name on a book, it was to share in it, all of it. And the most wonderful thing of all is that they also wanted to share in the success. We were doing it for each other, motivation for one and all.

Some people want to keep it to themselves, good luck if that's what drives them. For me it's a lonely conclusion, where do you take the va va voom? Me, I want to take success to the pub and be the first up to the bar. I want to be the person getting everyone to raise their glasses saying *I told you so, I knew we could do it*. I want to be the person to send everyone out of there with a purpose and a belief that they can do it, all of it, some of it but never none of it.

It's drive and determination that leads to inspiration and motivation. Out of one bar and into the next, another drink to life and what it can bring. And if writing this can take me out and about to talk to others and give them hope and inspiration, and the courage to believe they have something equally as valuable in themselves, then it's been a journey worth taken. For me that becomes even more motivating. There's no stopping this kid. I hope you fall over me soon, it'll prove I'm getting out more! Shakespeare was a good bloke, he got it right. *As you like it.* Damn right, I like it!

All the world's a stage, And all the men and women merely players.
They have their exits and their entrances, and one man in his time
plays many parts, His being seven ages.
—Shakespeare

What a guy, a dodgy frock and lacking a bit on the grooming but hell, he knew how to tell 'em. If I'm at a stage, let this be numero uno, and if it's the seventh let it be better than the sixth. To think he wrote that and never got a gig as a motivational speaker. Wouldn't it be worth 15,000 bucks for a weekend at his Alpine retreat where he motivated you? And bro, would I like to go to the book signing and have my picture taken with him!

But to be serious for once (seriously!) we are all on our stage, maybe for that one time, maybe others depending on our beliefs. The fact is, we need to make the most of what we have today. What we have is ourselves and each other. What we have is in all of us but sometimes we need to go look for it—our motivation. We need to have that surge of energy, that adrenalin rush that pushes us forward to do what we know we can do.

And if those around us don't have it quite as much, then maybe we need to reach out and help them, safe in the knowledge that one day you might need that helping hand…. that one person saying you can do it. I know you can do it. Now YOU need to know. You need to convince yourself you CAN do it. We can all be motivated at different times and at different levels, not a bad thing. That can mean that occasionally you're thinking it through and don't want to mouth off too much. I've been there and I've got a mouth! Sometimes it needs a thinking through and a little time with yourself so you can get it right in your head. Go on, *make a plan, Stan,* where you began, man to where you're go an. (I'm a poet, eh? Sloppy rhyme, I call it.) And when the time is right you might want to share it with a few people, family, friends who's opinions you value. Suddenly that enthusiasm is shared, and they love it. You're up and you're away and the time is right to tell others.

You've earned it

Motivation is your reward for all that belief. If I've said it before hang in there and read on 'cause I'm going to tell you again. If you think everything is stacked up against you, it isn't, think again. How you may *think it is*, lies just in your head. That's the one thing you need to address. It's never as bad as it appears, but *stinkin' thinkin'* can wear you down at times. Motivation is what excites and propels you forward and you need to keep it your main line of focus. You need to believe that you can overcome the obstacles especially when the going gets tough, and it will.

Enter once more the motivated person, the one person who can pick you up more than you can pick yourself up. Because they are motivated it's important for them to share their motivation with you and help you to persevere. Corners were made for turning, while you need approach them with caution, NEVER take the detour. The detour is a diversion, it's never the right way. It's someone else pointing you in a different direction and it isn't YOUR choice.

Paths of glory are paved with moments of indecision

Are they really? Paths are there for a reason. You need to sometimes tread a little more carefully and you may not want to take that road, at least not until you are sure. Motivated people maybe push out a little further, want to stride forward more purposefully, go a little faster. But it isn't recklessness, it's (once again) BELIEF. They are at a place in their head where they can only see a positive outcome, and they love being there. A person can still be motivated if they are a little more cautious. They might not be a risk taker, they may have too many everyday life commitments, family, food and fear of famine. It might appear irresponsible if they see that motivation itself is enough. It's where responsibility outweighs gusto. Good luck in where you go and who you go there with.

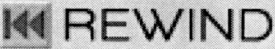 REWIND

MOTIVATION

1. **I**nspiration: It's is about the moment. Motivation is a constant.

2. **N**egativity: Never let circumstance quell your enthusiasm.

3. **S**imonism: The undisputed drive and ambition to maintain all levels of motivation and go where Cowell goes.

4. **P**rosperity: Can come from a positive approach to work and an undeniable passion for life.

5. **I**dentification: Find out what it is that motivates you and stay true to it.

6. **R**ally: Motivate one another. Pick each other up when the going gets tough. There is strength in numbers.

7. **E**ntertain: An enthusiastic workplace is infectious and a fun place to be. Let the creative juices flow.

CHAPTER 10

THE ART OF MANAGEMENT

I'M WITH THE BAND (GOD HELP YOU!)

The music business is a cruel and shallow money trench, a long plastic hallway where thieves and pimps run free and good men die like dogs. There's also a negative side.
—Hunter S. Thompson

You played in a band but you weren't really good enough so you thought, I'll become the manager. Wouldn't it be nice if it was that easy? That's what I did, well sort of. I was playing bass but we had another five guitarists and any one of them could have played bass far better than me. So I felt it my place to take rock and roll retirement, well as far as being a rock star anyway. I was the one with the connections too. I came up with the rehearsal room and negotiated the deal with my mum, as it was in our house. It kept me in the band though.

So you wanna be a rock and roll star

Back in the 60s anything to do with a band was cool. In my case, we weren't a working band and had no idea what a record deal was, so the management job wasn't really a job at all. But it did allow me to get us into my house for nothing. Even when I'd left, I managed to renegotiate an extended stay in the rehearsal room, still with the same terms.

Closely connected but miles apart

The days when the drummer's brother, sister's boyfriend or headmaster's son could manage you are long gone. It's not enough for them to be affable, if they screw up everyone becomes ostracized.

The manager's role in a band is a thankless task. Whenever a band becomes successful then it's all down to how brilliant they are and if they don't it's because you're a bad manager! At least if you speak to one of the band that's what they'll tell you. It's never that they just might be not good enough. There are also a great many stories of managers getting the sack just as the band is on the verge of success. That's when the sharks appear. Somebody whispers something in their ear, *Why do you need him (or her)? I can be your manager. We'll go places.* It happens all the time.

Expect the worse—it'll probably happen

If you ever get to manage a band make sure you have a good lawyer, no make that a GREAT lawyer. Expect the worse and it can only get better. There are plenty of books on how to manage but it's not a *how-to* business. You need to actually do it to understand it. You need to have labored, had sleepless nights and questioned why the hell you ever bothered. You need to have lost your patience, your understanding and probably your hair. That loss is the price of experience, something nothing or no one can ever teach you. That said, management today is vital to every part of the process, whether or not you have someone do it or you do it yourself. Rant over, read on.

Make a start, Do it yourself

There needs to be structure and there needs to be a plan. Where do I want to be in six months, a year? In five years? Think about it, if you don't know then no else is going to care. Think it over now and save everyone the hassle. Successful management needs to be the result of innovative thinking, collaboration and hard work. Throw creativity into the mix and you're on the way. It helps if your record company has half a brain, too.

If you can't find a manager who'll make a difference then you might as well do it yourself, at least for now. The amount of acts that are getting signed today has decreased drastically and record companies are only signing people who have built a solid base—and a solid base (bass) is not a rhythm section. It means doing it yourself. It's long and it's tiring but it's the only way you'll ever know what anyone thinks about you. DIY is now the best, most honest form of artist development.

It'd be very hard to find a manager of any substance prepared to take on the very arduous task of hustling everyone, and usually for no or minimal return. At this stage, if you want a manager with a reputation it's likely they'll be representing someone else as well and won't have the time. Someone has to make them some money and it's not you, at least today it isn't. With that said, it isn't easy and besides, they'll be plenty of people to hate soon enough, why add another.

Welcome to the real world, now be on your way

The music industry has changed radically and without good management it's very difficult to reach a high level of success. There are almost too many functions now for you to learn and with a rapidly changing business model it's about being one step ahead.

The shift of power has turned away from the record company and back to the artist. If you have strong leadership at management level today, you have much greater control over your career. The record company is no longer pulling the strings. At last you don't need them and if they do want you they'll have to pay for it. You've done all the legwork so whatever pockets they have left, let them dig deep. You've earned it.

Truly, madly, deeply—Great

You will rarely find a great artist without a great manager and the greatest managers are those who can build efficient and competent teams. Led Zeppelin had Peter Grant, U2 had Paul McGuiness and Matchbox Twenty have benefited from the expertise of Michael Lippman.

These and people like them are true legends from inside the engine room. Here are great managers at work with their creative artists. By building teams and helping to harness that creativity they end up with not only great acts but commercially successful ones too. While they need to get the most out of their artist, they also need to know how to deal with the side that borders between genius and total pain in the ass.

Juggling

It can be a fine balancing act to manage creative people. While creative people need to create, don't let them over create or mayhem sets in. They may have a talent but they don't have the right to disrupt what you are doing. You'll be working hard and likely be doing a great deal more.

126

They'll be writing (hopefully) and shagging (definitely). You don't need to go looking for your artist who may have gone AWOL because they've had a bad day.

Managing the creativity

Peter Grant worked his whole time with Led Zeppelin with just a hand shake deal. Often referred to by the band as the band's *fifth member* his style of management was total authoritarian. I admired him enormously for how he set the perimeters that others followed. He was a ferocious bull for his artists. He pioneered the artist being more powerful than the promoter by demanding ninety percent of the door from all their gigs. They had no choice, Led Zeppelin was always the hottest ticket in town. Peter Grant was aware ten percent of Led Zeppelin was worth more than ninety percent of most other bands anyway! Everyone was a winner.

The legacy remains

Working with Michael Lippman I saw the complete package. After a lifetime in management at the highest level he understands every part of the process. He's worked on the other side too as a lawyer, an agent and a record company head. He has all the answers to all the questions but what separates him from the rest is his unique understanding of human beings. And believe it or not artists fall in to that category, mostly.

I've probably put together more deals backstage at concerts than by telephone.
—Michael Lippman

Lippman observed that record producers and songwriters, artists in their own right, lacked proper career guidance. He started a management firm representing select performers and creating a business ensuring that all players in the creative process were protected and properly rewarded. Lippman was manager of George Michael, Matchbox Twenty, Bernie Taupin and others. That's the secret to the man's success. He doesn't manage from the boardroom. He's in the trenches with his troops. He manages the creativity by being constantly surrounded by it, understanding it and working with it. He doesn't have a preconceived idea of how it works or how somebody tells him it works. He sees it and he breathes it everyday. He is the prevention not the cure. He leads from the front, an unbelievable captain to have in your team.

Tell it like it is

Working with people like this is invigorating and inspirational, you are constantly learning but at the same time they are learning from you. They want to know what is happening with their artists and they want to know the truth. They are not afraid of bad news. They don't want you feeding some story to the record company about everything going well when there are problems. Whenever I needed help he was there with, *What can I do to help?* There are many more functions for the manager to perform now with so many revenue streams available to the artist. They need to be constantly searching for them.

As I previously mentioned, the shift of power is now firmly with the artist allowing them greater artistic control and the ability to make decisions internally without the interference of the record company. If the labels had their own way they would want to change that. With record sales declining year after year they are desperate to look for other income streams. Trying to get the artist to give away part of their income will not be easy. Especially for stuff like merchandising which they don't need a record company for anymore.

Beware the beast

Good managers have to be always looking, always watching. If the artist likes to drink, then don't have them work with an alcoholic record producer. It's hardly rocket science. Empowering the artist will give them confidence, it's the motivational weapon in their creative artillery. It propels them forward and it keeps them driven, focused and innovative. In giving them that confidence they must also be careful not to abuse it and start to feel superior.

Unleash the creative beast

Creative people need to be working with the right people in order to ensure that creativity is applied in the correct areas. The people doing that are the managers. It isn't necessarily about the manager being creative, it's more important that they are able to manage the creativity around them. They accomplish this by bringing in a team of creative people and encouraging them to collaborate.

The whole is greater than the parts where creative people work in tandem with non creative people. Whenever you see a creative person underachieve, just look around and you'll see they are working with the wrong people. Their creativity is minimal and their ideas nonexistent. Put them together with the right people and they are totally different. They will inspire and be inspired by those around them when ideas are abundant and creativity levels soar.

Stifling creativity

Some of the considerations to make when managing creative talent is to be able to understand what makes that individual creative. Writers might get *writers block* and not be able to work according to the timelines set by the record company. They may become dejected and their creativity levels could drop. Creative people work when creativity flows and not when the record company need products to meet quarterly targets.

Plague avoidance

A good manager is careful to keep his artist away from certain people, especially those at the record company they have taken a dislike to. If there is a particular person that your artist doesn't like, try to avoid situations where they are seated opposite each other at a dinner. Not good! I've seen it happen where I witnessed a record company executive (of high ranking) behave like an absolute jerk. Already unpopular with the artist he slowly, during the course of the evening got himself embarrassingly drunk. And we all know what utter hogwash transpires when the alcohol kicks in. He dug the hole that I so desperately wanted to lower him in to.

Where's my hit

The poor pop star was already there under extreme duress. *It'll be a good career move* was what his manager had told him but instead he had to endure an entire evening discussing why he hadn't written a hit single. I couldn't believe what I was hearing. I can only imagine what he said to his manager later. Later came a lot earlier after he feigned illness with a few excuse trips to the bathroom, the last one where he deliberately let out a sound of acute hurling to make it all the more convincing. Clearly it was put on

130

because if he had felt like puking, I think I know where he would have directed it.

Establishing the roles

When an artist appoints a manager it is vital they identify which roles they will be undertaking in order for the artist to do what they do best—write songs. Whatever they don't need to be doing, the manager needs to take care of and if that's not the case, they need to say so early in the relationship. The mere fact that they are creative people means that they have to be left alone to create and anything that involves business can usually add to the pressure.

Managing an act today

Managing relationships are so very important in modern management. In the music industry those types of relationships, be it the plugger with the manager, manager with the producer, the relationship of the producer with the band are crucial to the success of an act. A good manager is one who knows how to get the very best out of their artists and to do that they need to ensure that all relationships are nurtured correctly. If you don't have that you're wasting your time. Management is not a job you can play at. Today it needs to be more professional than ever.

Building a wall

Nowadays, since you need the artist to do so much for themselves, the role of manager has changed. At the top end you need a powerful, influential manager who can act as the buffer between the artist and the record company. Where the record company might want to exert their influence because they have money invested, the manager can ensure they are protecting their act. Record companies will want to pressure them to deliver records to meet their projected quarterly targets. Successful acts are their lifeline (remember the friendly dinner story). No good manager would allow that but would still need to offer an explanation if a recording was delayed. At the other end of the scale when the act is unknown it is difficult to secure good management.

Who the hell are you

An unknown manager without a reputation is going to find it hard to get to record companies. Today's companies are signing fewer and fewer artists and they rarely listen to unsolicited material. What that effectively means is, if they don't know you they won't listen to what you have. In defense of the labels, they simply don't have the resource to wade through endless CDs, most of which are crap.

Practice Golden-Rule 1 of Management in everything you do.
Manage others the way you would like to be managed.
—Brian Tracy

Sometimes though, managing creativity can be totally invigorating. Artists can be wonderful human beings. They can be pleasant, jolly creative, interesting and fun to be with, and there are times when they are not. You end up being their mother, their brother, their sister and their dad. One such beast pissed me off so much that I went outside the TV studio and scribbled down these words, just for him!

Artistic translation

Driven..................Driving you mad

Creative................Creating mayhem

Imaginative............On another planet

Prolific..................A total pain in the ass

Confident..............Swagger, arrogance

Far out..................Further the better!

Adventurous...........Meandering, a wanderer

Innovative.............In one ear, out the other

Sexy.....................Predatory

Pensive.................Insecure

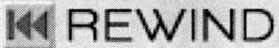 REWIND

THE ART OF
MANAGEMENT

1. Building: A foundation for good management is having the right people around you.

2. Energy: Time management and a demanding schedule, be sure you're cut out for it.

3. Lawyer: Get one! Sign nothing until someone who knows has looked at your agreement.

4. Innovation: Original thinking, collaboration and hard work are crucial to successful management.

5. Experience: Accept no substitute, it's where knowledge begins and ends.

6. Vitality: Drive is the most vital of all management skills along with commitment.

7. Eccentrics: The world is full of them. Learn to deal with the different personalities you will encounter.

CHAPTER 11

INTERPERSONAL SKILLS
KNOW HOW, WHAT, WHEN AND WHY TO DO IT

Before you criticize someone
be sure to walk a mile in their shoes. Then if you still choose to
criticize them they're a mile away and you have their shoes!
—Eleanor Roosevelt (well the first part anyway!)

How much time you get to spend with someone will depend on their schedule and how much time they want to spend with you. Don't hang around debating last night's American Idol and making inane conversation. Say what you have to say and go. If there is anything else they want from you they'll happily call and ask and if they don't just be glad you left.

Never outstay your welcome

Remember the names of the people you meet. It shows you're a listener. Always know as much as you can about the person you are talking to and especially the job they do. The more you know about them the easier it will be to understand them and work out the best way to deal with them. They'll have a particular way they want you to deal with them and whether it's e-mail, telephone, carrier pigeon. Do it. Yours is not to question why.

Share your knowledge with others.

Having experience in any job is a huge plus but be careful how you use it. The one thing I valued as much as anything in all my years in the music business was the opportunity I had to learn from others. From the day you start, everybody you meet is more experienced than you, even if they only started a day earlier. I was fortunate enough to have mentors, people I met along the way that taught me so much. Good mentors are a huge asset. They are people who have proved themselves and now want to share that knowledge. I've found them to be both inspirational and motivating, the ones who always have time for you. Whenever possible, I would try to do the same. If someone asks something of you it's a compliment. It means they value your opinion and are interested in what you have to say. Take the time to give the time.

The people you meet on the way up are the same people you meet on the way down

In the first few months and just as I was learning the promotion *techniques* I received my own baptism of fire! I had the unenviable task of working with a band who were about to release the follow up to their recent hit. Lucky me I thought, the follow up to a Top Five single. This should be easy. I couldn't have been more wrong. These guys thought they were invincible. They thought they were famous pop stars. How sadly mistaken they were, one top five record doesn't make you famous. It makes you known—for a few weeks anyway.

Everybody's watching

Instant success is a very important time for an artist or band as everybody is keenly watching their progress. TV wants to book them, radio wants to play them and girls want to shag them. What else could a guy want, a brain maybe? Well for me a little decency, respect and professionalism goes a long way. Possibly it was too much too soon? Bollocks, it's the manager's job to deal with that. That one instance left a lasting impression on me, I thought, *amateurs* and when they fell from grace I couldn't care less. Sad because I can't remember anyone else it happened to, yet it happened with the first band I ever worked with in PR! Fortunately for me it didn't set the pattern as most of the artists saw the need to be polite and courteous. Half a brain tells you if you want to get along in business, be nice to people.

Keep your own house in order

Work as a team. Integrating and meeting regularly with your staff is paramount. It doesn't always have to be of a formal nature and sometimes just sitting around a desk or over a cup of coffee can suffice. And if business is good you each get to have a cup. Running your own company is like being the landlord of a pub. People won't drink there if they don't see you behind the bar five nights a week. Your staff will work harder if they see you are in the office more than out on the golf course. Funny really, if you're pissed people can tell.

Man the building

I was always first in and unless I had somewhere to go, last out. If I was out of the office then it was a given that someone would always be there to open up. Invariably it was my right hand man, Lee and I would never have to ask him, he just did it. It's vitally important for your clients and work colleagues to know what time your office is open. I have always hated voicemail. When you need to reach somebody and you need an answer, all you get is—nowhere!

Lead by example

I knew people who ran promotion companies who would close up early on a Friday if it was quiet. You can bet the call you missed at the end of the day would be from an important manager or radio programmer. Maybe someone wanting to book a band at the very last minute and the opportunity is gone. For some very busy people this may be the only time they can call, the only free moment they've had all day. Heads of Promotion would call first thing because they knew I'd be there. If they were stuck in traffic they'd call and because they were away from the distractions of the office the conversations were better. We'd have more time to go over things as well as discuss last night's football, imperative to good bonding. It meant there was less for them to attend to when they got to work and it was also of great help to me. If it was a matter of importance, I could feed the information directly to my staff when they arrived. We'd share that big cup of coffee.

Share the information

The more information they have the better they are able to do their job. Involving others and sharing your ideas and plans with your staff helps to keep them motivated. Allow them to share in the success and help with the problems. If you are driving the project it's always beneficial to have extra eyes and ears and for others to be objective. When you get too attached to the project your outlook gets blinkered. Don't be anal. It's counter productive and creatively obstructive. If you want to criticize someone or something then make sure you offer constructive criticism. It's better to say *have you thought of doing it this way?* than *That won't work.* Everyone has shoes, wear them!

Look out for others and they'll look out for you

The more you work with someone the more you get to know about them. You'll know when something is wrong or if they have personal problems. There may be health issues, financial problems and the like. Everyone has lives, and while it isn't any of your business, it is your business to ask if you sense there is something wrong. Some may feel they're on their own and could use someone to talk to, others might not. Don't interfere but let them know you're there and willing to help. There is nothing better than fellow workers showing compassion. Everyone likes to know they're working with human beings and it doesn't matter if you're a colleague or their boss. Just ask if you can help. If they don't want you to help they'll say so but that one time could be the time they really need it.

Show you care

While you can't help with any health issues, if you're their boss you may be able to loan them some money or advance them a pay check. It isn't the money, it's having someone know they care. The more you know about people the more understanding you can be about circumstances and more willing to help. Unexpected pressures can mount and something as simple as giving them an afternoon off can go a long way.

Do unto others

If you treat people the way you'd like to be treated you'll find them easier to get along with. Loyal relationships are imperative. They get you through work and they get you through life. If things are going well there are people to share it with and if you're feeling low you don't have to carry the burden on your own.

Work that room

Networking is as important now as it's ever been. If you're constantly around and meeting people it keeps your name out there. It only takes someone to say *Guess who I saw yesterday?* and your profile is raised or your reputation enhanced! No technology can ever replace the interaction one human being has with another. The eyes have it! My entire life was built on relationships. I found meeting new people was a huge advantage. I was fantastic and they had a right to know! Confident people are assertive. They don't have problems with ego and they're not out to try and impress. They are liked because they're normal. Normal is good, try it. Social networking is the new paradigm and a new way to inter-personalize your skills. It's a whole new ballgame, a new way to do business. And there's probably many more books to read on the subject.

Walk this way

Working with a wide cross-section of artists for many years, it was easy to see who the media were most interested in. Some rock stars think they have something to live up to, they like to swagger. If they piss you off, they'll piss off the people you have to deal with. That's a REAL pisser. They have that look of disdain when they'd rather be somewhere else and are incapable of hiding it. It can be intimidating for everybody and it's your job to address it. If you sense the prima donna creeping in then face the situation head on. This may be someone who you worked with right from the start when they were nobody. Remind them when they were no one and that next time around when they're no one again, NO ONE WILL GIVE A FUCK.

He who shouts the loudest is often heard the least

Those who are belligerent and obnoxious are to be avoided. They feel that shouting gets them heard. Getting heard and being noticed are two entirely different things. People who scream and shout probably get the runaround at home and come to work pissed off with a need to vent their fury. Unfortunately, it's usually some quiet unassuming person that bares the brunt of it. There are also the times when artists or clients may be acting out of character. Work it out in your head before you start on theirs. Have you seen them behaving better? Good, then it's uncharacteristic. More importantly, if it's happening more often than not, then it's starting to become characteristic. You need to nip it in the bud and pronto. Pressures can mount up and you need to be able to identify the problem. It may not be terminal, you might be able to fix if you detect it early.

Fading friends

Take them aside and start with the line, *You used to be great to work with.* Stop, pause, and then slowly start to walk away. Are you getting a reaction? Do they look slightly puzzled? Do they look at all concerned? If they are standing motionless, you planted the seed. Now it's for them to realize you are only trying to help. However, if they don't appear to respond or look like they care it's the beginning, of the end.

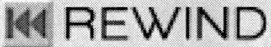 **REWIND**

INTERPERSONAL SKILLS

1. Prima donna syndrome: Meet them head on, if you don't they'll walk all over you.

2. E.S.P: Extra sensory perception. The more you know someone the better equipped you'll be to deal with them.

3. Rapport: Encourage dialogue with people but more importantly learn how to sustain that dialogue.

4. Social Networking: The new paradigm, and the new way to inter-personalize your skills.

5. Obstacles: Share information with colleagues and staff. Being open will encourage and inspire them.

6. Nuisance: A continually pushy person, disrespectful of other peoples schedules.

7. Authenticity: Be yourself, everyone likes the real thing.

8. Loyalty: Relationships flourish when you are trusted. It will get you through work and it will get you through life.

9. Integrate: Meet with staff or the people you work with regularly.

10. Tenacity: Some people can test your perseverance. Be patient.

11. YMCA: Yes Mentors Can Assist. We all need mentors. Choose them well and go on to mentor others.

CHAPTER 12

COLLABORATION

JOIN TOGETHER WITH THE BAND

One life you gotta do what you should.

One life with each other, sisters, brothers. But we're not the same we

get to carry each other, carry each other.

—U2

Collaboration has been a constant in the music industry for as long as I can remember. People have always collaborated. It's the one thing the business was good at and even though it can lead to the inevitable power struggle it still leaves it's legacy. Without the willingness to collaborate so much of what became successful never could have been. It's that simple.! Great minds do think alike when they're allowed to collaborate. One person's idea can be the inspiration for someone else to implement and execute the idea. When an individual learns to collaborate, over a period of time they become serial collaborators, always looking for new people to collaborate with.

The desire to collaborate is the road to success

You can go back to the 50s with songwriting partnerships like Rodgers and Hammerstein, Lieber and Stoller, Gamble and Huff and of course a little later Lennon and McCartney. The music industry has had some of it's greatest successes from the result of collaborations. You can say that now

143

with the rappers it's as powerful as it's ever been. An established artist such as Jay Z will use his success and influence to start his own record label. He'll find a young talented rapper and have them collaborate with an established artist or producer. Such is the fan base for someone with Jay Z's pedigree that the acceptance is immediate and that fledgling artist can become a million-selling superstar overnight.

Coming together is a beginning.
Keeping together is progress. Working together is success.
—Henry Ford

It isn't even restricted to the collaboration of rappers with other rappers, just look at Dido. She became a multi-platinum act after Eminem recruited her to guest on one of his early tracks. She sang a chorus that became so identifiable that a whole career beckoned. She was signed and as the saying goes, the rest was history!

Go back even further. A classic example of collaboration was Run DMC and Aerosmith. Run DMC was a credible, successful rap act who quite honestly didn't need Aerosmith, but their career had started to wane and album sales were on the decline. The resulting collaboration, *Walk this way* became a rock standard and suddenly a new audience arrived for the veteran rockers.

The beauty of collaboration is that you have different styles of music and artists who bring different creative ideas to the table. All of a sudden, it just gels. Commercially, they start to cross over and sell to each others core fan base of rappers and rockers. This becomes mutually beneficial in profiling both acts and yet doesn't always require the need to go back and do it again. Doing it once is seen as innovative. The second time around it may not work. When the smarter acts catch on they still collaborate, just not always with the same people.

Every collaboration helps you grow. With Bowie, it's different every time. I know how to create settings, unusual aural environments. That inspires him. He's very quick.
—Brian Eno

Collaboration in the recording studio has always been popular and again some of the most significant records of the last few decades resulted from the teaming up of creative minds. Take Brian Eno with David Bowie and *Low* and Daniel Lanois and Eno for U2's *The Joshua Tree*, the album that catapulted U2 in to the stratosphere and a complete departure from their previous records. Good producers working with good engineers, always bring new insight on various ways of working with the artists and give the project an innovative dimension. The collaboration doesn't even begin and end in the studio but at it's inception. When a record company A&R person teams up an artist with a particular producer, they approach both parties and recommend they work together. It's what A&R's role used to be—the ability to sit back and offer constructive criticism when an artist is too close to their own work.

Corroborate to collaborate

Managing creativity is undoubtedly where collaboration can be seen working effectively in the music industry. Artist development, the thing closest to my heart and the reason we even have heroes, was always about collaboration on all levels. The manager would collaborate with their artist to maximize creativity. By delegating, they took away the unnecessary obligations which could be better served by other members within the team. Individual roles and tasks were spread around. A multitasking artist, is an unhappy artist! Let them do what they do best, write and/or perform. The manager is the conduit and the chief collaborator, the person most likely to team up person A with person B. Once the collaboration is in place they are in the best position to manage the process for the duration. After all they brought the culprits in and if any problems arise it's for them to mediate and resolve issues—and live happily ever after!

That's just the way it is.

—Bruce Horsby

Collaboration is everywhere in business today. It's the whole Wiki theory where businesses are not only encouraged to collaborate with their customers but with their competitors too. Don Tapscott's book *Wikinomics* is a fascinating read where he writes that mass collaboration changes everything.

Today 330 million people use Wikipedia as their online source for knowledge. Compare the meager eight years of their existence to previous generations that used the Encyclopedia Britannica as their bible. If anything needed to be changed in Britannica it had to wait until the following year's edition. Wikipedia is so up-to-date that if anything changes it's changed that day, and usually by several outside contributors. An encyclopedia for the people by the people. Incredible!

Why beat them when you can join them

Collaboration has become the buzz word today. You really know it's working when technology companies team up with one another to become a greater force. They combine their massive strengths with one

146

another to become a formidable enterprise. Why bother taking each other on and take years to understand what they do better than you. Now it's the accepted norm and will continue to be so. Those thinking in a forward manner are those less likely to get left behind.

In the workplace as with the music industry different skills come together to provide a better service or product. In the music industry it isn't rocket science to identify who the best people for the job are. If you are an independent promoter then the artist or their manager needs to decide if you are the right person for the job. Someone may be right for one act but totally wrong for another. When you team up with the right PR person, the collaboration begins. Whatever each one achieves benefits the other. If the record is on the radio it's easier to get press and if the group or artist is on the radio (or TV) then it gives them something to talk to the press about. And if you get neither, generally you're fucked. Or you used to be, nowadays you can be your own publicist and do a lot more. But that's another book!

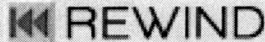 REWIND

COLLABORATION

1. Producer: Collaborates with artist to provide a creative and innovative product.

2. Alliance: Form one to begin the collaboration.

3. Rappers: Some of the greatest of all collaborators.

4. Team: Great minds think alike when they collaborate.

5. Niche: Experiment with each other's uniqueness.

6. Encourage: Persuade colleagues to collaborate with competitors.

7. Rejuvenate: Reviving old trends with new ideas. You got it right, it's all about collaboration!

CHAPTER 13

MISTAKES

COCK UPS AND BLUNDERS
OOPS, I DID IT AGAIN!

Mistakes are the portals of discovery.

—James Joyce

That's most definitely one of my favorite quotes. Those few words help you to understand the logic behind making a mistake. How will you ever learn anything if you don't risk trying?

Mistakes open your eyes to discovery and with that the opportunity to succeed. Successful people succeed as a result of the chances they take and the mistakes they make. They aren't afraid of failure, the same fear of failure that prevents others from taking risks. Those that have made mistakes are twice as likely to risk making more. Many entrepreneurs, Richard Branson being one, have failed several times. You don't think successful people fail but they do. The difference is they don't see it as failure, more as something of value. For some there is a stigma attached to failure. They see it as embarrassment. That should never be the case.

I'll try anything once.

—Richard Branson

Where is the shame in taking a risk, in showing that you are prepared to take a chance? I personally admire the risk takers. As long as the risk is an opportunity there is always the chance to succeed. As you manage creativity you also need to allow people to fail. Always be trying to do something with someone, somehow and not worry if it does fail. As creative people learn from failure, so will you. Embrace those mistakes and realize that the most important lesson you can learn from a mistake is the experience itself. Creative failure can bring with it resilience and a desire to succeed.

The first mistake is to never think you've made one and once you've made one you'll only wish you made one sooner. So what if you do fail? If you've haven't failed then you haven't taken enough risks. It's not whether you get knocked down, it's whether you get back up again.

Take a chance, make a mistake

Making a mistake says a lot about your character to both your colleagues and your competitors. It shows you have a great deal of courage. It show's you are creative and innovative and you're willing to try something different. U2 have made more than their fair share of mistakes all through their career. Almost always there has been a positive outcome.

Let's look at two remarkable events that had an enormous impact on the band's future. Each time it could have spelled disaster but their willingness to fail carried them through.

It's a beautiful day

U2's singer Bono made an almighty blunder in 1985 during the band's performance at Live Aid which ended up as their *Beautiful Day*. Live Aid was THE major global music event of the 80s, a once in a lifetime experience with an audience of 1.4 billion. You couldn't blame anyone for being nervous.

U2 prepared for their brief set by going over the order of the songs meticulously. Meanwhile, Bob Geldof was adamant that no band, whoever they were, would be allowed longer than fifteen minutes and for U2 that amounted to three songs.

With so many other performances on different stages all over the world, it was a logistical nightmare. There was no room to compromise for anyone.

With the world watching

The concert kicked off at Wembley Stadium in London and from there it later linked up via satellite to JFK Stadium in Philadelphia. Through a stroke of genius, U2 had negotiated to be the first band America would see when they tuned in, guaranteeing them a prestigious slot.

Everything started really well until the second song *Bad* when Bono decided to walk down past the cameras and pull a girl from the crowd. This wasn't in the plan and their tour manager was forced to follow him holding the trailing microphone lead. Bewilderment!

Let's dance

Down on the lowest platform at the very front of the stage, he reached out, pulled a girl from the crowd and started to slow dance with her. It was his way of connecting with this huge audience both in the stadium and all around the world. It was a beautiful gesture and a very tender moment, but in reality it also meant there was no time for the third song. The band was looking round while continuing to play, wondering where their lead singer had disappeared to. Their fifteen glorious minutes were now up and the plug was pulled. The band put down their instruments, managed a wave and sloped off the stage seething.

The inevitable conclusion is rarely the original plan

The band and their manager were furious. They thought they'd blown it because they didn't get to play the single *Pride* the one song most people knew.

This was their big chance. A golden opportunity on a global stage, all they ever wanted and Bono had blown it. What the hell was he thinking? The band couldn't understand it and prone as he (Bono) was to doing the unexpected, why would he have done this today of all days? They had discussed everything beforehand, aware of the time restrictions and how there was no room for error.

Off stage there was complete silence as heads hung low. Bono was distraught thinking he had let everyone down and returned to Ireland to hideaway at a friend's house. Their manager, Paul McGuinness, went off to France totally pissed off at the opportunity his singer had squandered.

You would never believe how close the band came to sacking Bono that day and how close they were to calling it quits. The following day, Paul went out for a newspaper and couldn't believe his eyes. All the press were unanimous, U2 had stolen the show! They had officially arrived. Now everyone knew who they were.

You would never equate U2 with failure, yet you can see how hovering on the brink of failure can take you to the pinnacle of success. Bono has learned from every mistake and for him it was probably all part of growing up. That willingness to fail has always been there. This mistake had turned into the greatest opportunity.

There are mistakes and then there are almighty mistakes. Some you would think would take a lifetime to recover from.

We don't like their sound.
Groups with guitars are on the way out.
—Dick Rowe (Decca Records)

Why Rowe passed on The Beatles in 1962 we'll never know. Somehow you doubt that would be on his resume. While mistakes are the portals of discovery, you wouldn't want that guy in charge of discovering your bands. Or would you?

Believe it or not he recovered from that almighty blunder and learned his lesson. The following year, Mr. Rowe admitted he didn't want to make the same mistake twice and promptly exonerated himself by signing The Rolling Stones to Decca, albeit on the recommendation of one George Harrison.

Learning from your mistakes

A common mistake people make is thinking they don't make mistakes. They think they are always right. Utter bollocks, who is ever always right? And he who thinks he is right is wrong thinking they're always right. They made a mistake just thinking they were right, right. Part of the problem is their resistance and their arrogance in being unprepared to admit they failed. To them admitting a mistake signifies failure. Their mistake lies in the assumption that they can't fail and has nothing to do with anything going wrong. The only thing going wrong is the mistake in their head.

The greatest opportunities can come from biggest mistakes

We all make mistakes, but how many of us learn from them? Whatever mistake you might make, try and understand how you came to make it. Dick Rowe did. Remember, the greatest education can be the result of one simple mistake.

My heroes are the ones who survived by doing it wrong,
who made mistakes but recovered from them.
—Bono

You know he's dead right too, my heroes have been the ones who made mistakes and I bet if you think about it yours have been too. They don't have to be heroes in the true sense of the word either, they could have been your peers, parents or mentors. The real value of those people is that they are the ones who are the most likely to admit to their failings. Or are they failings? Just because the outcome wasn't what you had in mind remember what the song and dance man told us.

If there's no success like failure then failure's no success at all

The difference is that those of us who have failed feel it's important to mention that we have failed. Remember again how Mr. Success himself experienced failure many times, wasn't his name Simon Cowell? He wasn't afraid to mention failure many times in his own book and if that doesn't inspire you nothing will. By the way this is about heroes and I just want to clarify that while Simon Cowell is certainly not a hero of mine, I have a great deal of admiration for what he's done. He's a good bloke and good luck to him. Like he needs me to wish him good luck!

When I was growing up Neil Young was (still is) a hero of mine yet he would never rest on his laurels. He was forever trying new things and not worrying about their commercial success if they satisfied his creative urgings. He had massive success with his *Harvest* album and the subsequent smash hit single *Heart of Gold*.

It made him a big star and he could have made a follow up that would have sold millions. Most people would do just that, record a follow up in much the same manner and sell to the already converted, but not our Neil.

Well not entirely true, there was *Harvest Moon*, the sister album to *Harvest*. But because of all his musical explorations in between it took twenty years for the follow up to be finally released, yet it still sounded just as fresh.

Okay, tell me I'm biased, but for me that is the true meaning of the word artist. They stretch their creativity and they're always ready for their next mistake because they see the plus in what might happen. If they don't try something then they will never be fulfilled. It's better for them to focus in

155

their songwriting than start abusing drugs. In some instances, it might be better to miss what you never had!

I have a theory that the only original things
we ever do are mistakes.
—Billy Joel

Mistake or opportunity

For some there is no such thing as failure, as mentioned in Bono's quote. Come in Mr. Song and dance man, Bob Dylan. After being the spokesman for a generation, a troubadour, a folkie, he went electric and in my old hometown, actually!

He appeared in Manchester one night in the mid sixties and played all the numbers people had grown up loving but with a band, *The Band.* And one guy in the audience famously jeered *Judas!* Dylan was betraying no one except himself if he didn't take that chance. He was never worried if people saw it as a mistake—he knew better.

Where some might call it mistake others might prefer to use the words innovative, creative or risk-taking. Whichever way you look at it the word mistake still seems so final. But as James Joyce told us at the beginning of the chapter *Mistakes ARE the portals of discovery.* And why not repeat that glorious message, it's the greatest lesson you'll ever learn and it's made even better because it's the lesson you taught yourself.

As Blurtit.com (an online community with all the answers) explains, usually the word *discovery* is used in reference to explorers and philosophers. (I love it because those types are heroes of mine!)

There's a subtle difference between the word *discovery* and *invention*. Invention happens when someone creates something, a scientist creates something for the very first time. In discovery, the place or thing is already there, waiting to be explored or found out.

For example, we know that Vasco da Gama discovered the *Cape of Good Hope*. This does not imply that he created that place, it was there, he merely explored and found that place. Discovery means to bring to light or *unearth*. So how on earth can you do it?

That's how. Make a mistake, discover it, unearth it and then go forward and make things happen.

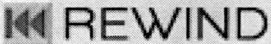 REWIND

MISTAKES

1. **E**ncouragement: Allow people to fail, it's nothing to be ashamed about.

2. **R**ealization: The most important lesson you can learn from mistakes is the mistake itself.

3. **R**ecovery: It's not whether you get knocked down it's whether you get back up again.

4. **O**verload: If you are constantly making mistakes maybe you want to look at yourself. You may be over stretching yourself and your expectations.

5. **R**etribution: What you gain from mistakes. Identify where you went wrong and don't make the same mistake twice.

6. **S**elf Esteem: Successful people have failed many times, don't let failure affect your confidence.

CHAPTER 14

INNOVATION

THE TIMES THEY ARE A CHANGIN'

If you're not failing every now and again,
it's a sign you're not doing anything very innovative.
—Woody Allen

These immortal lines from Bob Dylan in 1963 have never rung truer. It's also a great excuse for me to litter his lyrical genius throughout this chapter.

Come gather 'round people, wherever you roam and admit that the
waters around you have grown....
Come mothers and fathers, throughout the land
And don't criticize what you don't understand
Your sons and your daughters are beyond your command
Your old road is rapidly aging'
Please get out of the new one if you can't lend your hand
For the times they are a changin'

The old road IS rapidly aging and everything we do from this day forward will be driven by innovative ideas and innovative thinking. It is now more important than ever to be aware of the change in the way people do business. In order to compete and increase efficiency they need to be constantly evolving. It is the innovators who move business forward by constantly creating new ways to reinvent themselves, their products, how they sell, market and promote.

The ideas we have today form the basis for the progress we make tomorrow

I don't think I had a clue at the time but when I was a kid growing up in the north of England the people who inspired me the most were the innovators. I doubt back then I even knew the meaning of the word but there was just something about the type of people who took chances that I admired.

Later on, I discovered that all my heroes were innovators. From artists like Neil Young to Bob Dylan, The Beatles, Frank Zappa, Captain Beefheart, Pink Floyd to the master chameleon himself, David Bowie, arguably the most innovative artist of our time and a totally fascinating subject on his own. Stick around, we'll come back to Bowie a little later.

These artists and others like them were constantly challenging themselves and constantly evolving. They are masters of reinvention. Innovation is what keeps an artist relevant in such a competitive market. There are those that have made it who think they have deserved it and all they need to do is release something new and the masses will come flocking. And there are those that succeed by always being one step ahead of the rest. In the music business, you are only ever as good as your last record. The public is fickle, fail to grab their attention anymore and they lose interest. You're history. The innovative thinkers whether at the label or in the band will know only too well what is required. It will take teamwork and fresh new ideas. Record labels sense weakness. If they don't see that you are in control of your own destiny, they'll do it for you. They'll plan every move and choose every single. They'll tell you when to release your albums, when to go on tour. They'll take over managing you and start to make the decisions that you've proved you can't.

It is the business of the future to be dangerous.
—Alfred North Whitehead

Innovation should come from the artist and through their management. The artist needs to be constantly collaborating with their manager and coming up with new ideas. Each needs to keep the other focused and working toward deadlines. If you come up with an idea for a new producer before the record company finds you one, you better have a good reason why you chose them.

Inspiration from Innovation

David Bowie has been described as the most influential artist of the century. I had been working with RCA for several years promoting his records to radio and television and in 1997 I was offered the chance to go on tour with him as his publicist. I had been a fan all my life and to be given this opportunity with an artist of such caliber was indeed a huge honor.

The way the whole business of Bowie operates is so amazingly efficient. It's his ideas and his vision that is complemented by having like minded individuals around him to help provide what he needs to make it work. He overseas the whole process but he allows people to breathe, even to make mistakes. David Bowie taught me that you can be hands on by keeping your hands off.

Innovation lessons learned

The American Heritage Dictionary defines innovation as *the act of introducing something new*. To me that IS David Bowie. His whole career has been one of innovation. Even at the tender age of thirteen he had a pretty good idea of where he wanted to be. At age twenty-two Bowie said that by the time he was thirty he would be a millionaire and spend the rest of his life doing other things. By the time he was thirty, he had released twelve albums, twenty-five singles and made his first film, *The man who fell to earth*. On John Lennon's recommendation, Bowie had taken control of his own career, dispensing with managers and setting up his own group of companies in Switzerland.

My favorite thing is to go where I've never gone.
—Dianne Arbus

He created his own ISP, like AOL, an internet service provider. He formed a corporation with an initial public offering (IPO) where he sold shares of himself and his catalogue of music. By consolidating the value of his copyright, he has amassed a fortune of somewhere in the region of six-hundred-million. David thinks of himself as a brand, a corporate entity, a platform and a change agent. If he limited himself to the traditional realm of musician then people would probably not be talking about him today.

Rebel, Rebel

I remember London, 1973. David Bowie was the biggest rock star on the planet and his *Ziggy Stardust* persona was the very icon of the Glam Rock era. One night was a defining moment for me though it didn't seem so at the time. It was the closing night of the tour and I was overwhelmed by the sheer magnitude of the performance. At the end of the show he banished the legend that was *Ziggy Stardust*. He broke up the band. I looked up at him from the third row, my mouth wide open. I was devastated, you're doing what!

That was the night I left a concert hall very pissed off. Turns out that Bowie needed a character to unleash the creative beast within him. Playing a character allowed him to do the things that he, as David Jones (his real name) just could not do. He had moved on from Ziggy and was already dreaming where his alter ego would take us next.

You can't stay the same. If you're a musician and a singer, you have to change, that's the way it works.

—*Van Morrison*

Then twenty-five years later when I ended up working with him I felt like I owed him an apology. If he hadn't have done what he'd done, I for one certainly wouldn't have had the privilege of working with him. His audience would have become bored and moved on and he'd just have been another x-pop star.

Bowie as that chameleon, has had many different personas apart from Ziggy. He has also had many emulators, some with greater success than others but there has been no successor. I doubt there ever will be. He has defined himself with more variety and flair than any of his contemporaries and that is why he is known as the most innovative artist of our time.

The line it is drawn, the curse it is cast
The slow one now will later be fast
As the present now will later be past

The order is rapidly fadin'
And the first one now will later be last
For the times they are a changin'

What is now proven was once someone's idea. The innovators are the creators of ideas and without ideas business would stand still. It's the same with rock and roll. Tired old songs won't inspire people.

Artists need to keep evolving, taking chances. For businesses to compete and to increase efficiency, they need to be constantly evolving. A lack of ideas show a lack of direction and you'll only have yourself to blame if you don't think ahead. If you are in a band, you are going to have to reinvent the dream. It was yours after all, so know what to do with it.

It may have been right for the time and what got you signed but it might be dated now. If you didn't see it coming it'll hit you like a ten wheeler, and you'll fall. The progress you make will be governed by the new ideas you have along the way. Those new ideas come in the songwriting— naturally that needs to evolve. Maybe it'll be in a new live show. Going out on tour needs to be thought out constantly, if people have seen you before they will expect something different and those who come to see you for the first time will need a reason to come back.

In the old days it was accepted that bands needed time to develop. How many times have you heard people mention *that crucial third album?* Today there are no such luxuries. A label will have dropped you well before then, more likely straight after the first album if it doesn't reach expectations.

In business, in leisure, in music and in entertainment you will see the results from innovation. The world moves at a pace where more than ever we need to keep up or we'll be left behind. Today technology moves by the minute, new ideas, new methods, new systems and new ways of doing things. All this applies to business as much as it does to making music. It's about how well we do things not how fast we do them.

Never try something just for the sake of it but try doing it in different ways with different ideas, different technology and with different people. And allow yourself to make different mistakes.

As innovation continues it will evolve in ways we don't always understand, in directions we can't always see and from people we don't even know. Embrace every new idea like it's the last one you'll ever have. Seek as much knowledge from your competitors as your colleagues and share that knowledge with others. Challenge what you don't understand and never be afraid to ask. Wisdom comes from questions, not from answers.

Accept advice and advise acceptance. Innovation requires a sense of adventure, a willingness to try something new. It's not a fad. It's not a fashion. It's where innovators position themselves at the forefront of creativity and at the frontline of invention. They are the true pioneers and they are forging the way forward, for us all.

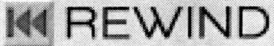 REWIND

INNOVATION

1. Redefine: Where you are today is not where you want to be tomorrow.

2. Evolution: It's the only solution.

3. Invention: And reinvention, the mother of all innovation.

4. Newness: Fresh ideas advance us in ways we don't always understand. Try different things with different people.

5. Variation: Create a mix of tried and tested methods with new and innovative ones.

6. Enthusiasm: Approach the desire to change with optimism.

7. Neverland: A place in your head but not a reality. Creative ideas need to be a possibility and not a pipedream.

8. Timing: Make the changes before you're forced to. Always be one step ahead of the pack.

CHAPTER 15

THE CELEBRITY FACTOR

FAME AND THE NAMELESS GAME

The price you pay for your riches and fame,

was it all a strange game, you're a little insane.

The money, the fame and the public acclaim,

don't forget who you are.

You're a rock and roll star.

—The Byrds

Andy Warhol's now legendary quote from the late sixties has come back to haunt us, *In the future everyone will be famous for fifteen minutes*. It's something he has regretted saying ever since, so much in fact that he re- interprets it whenever he has the chance! You could hold him partly responsible for helping to create the reality world that we live in. Reality mayhem! But in the 60s, who wouldn't have wanted to be Lennon, Dylan, Hendrix or Bowie?

Andy Warhol eat your heart out

Warhol couldn't be David Bowie or Iggy Pop so he invented the *fifteen minutes* as his calling card. In doing so, he also gave these wannabes the lifeline they so desperately crave. A minute of fame would be more than ample for most of them.

Famous or fortunate

What a sad reflection on life and how dissatisfied people must be, why else would you want to suffer the indignation of making a complete fool of yourself in front of total strangers? Playing the fool is a wonderful pastime that should be enjoyed after a few drinks and in the company of close friends—and then left there! The real fun comes the following morning when you have to face those same friends and be told what exactly it was you had done.

A wannabe celebrity will do absolutely anything if there's a chance for them to be on television or in the papers. They think that if they're on television they're famous but they're not, they're confused. They are mixing up fame with notoriety.

Their constant craving for attention means they are willing to risk everything whatever the consequences.

Playing the fame game

Apart from Warhol's flippant comment, celebrity fallout may have started with Big Brother and just never really gone away. With each reality TV series the producers encourage a little more outrage and a little more daring hoping to push the risqué a little further. Doing this keeps everyone happy. It gives the television shows the chance for higher ratings and it allows the contestants the opportunity to be seen by more people, most of whom probably think they're jerks anyway! Sex sells, whoever's selling it.

Anti Star Wars

For every media whore desperate to be famous, the stars with the real talent aren't willing to be part of that circus anymore. Instead, they go about their daily routine coming out to attend the awards ceremonies where they are recognized for their achievements and by their peers. If the media can't tempt them, their profession still can. The real star is quickly becoming the anti-star.

Wealth and fame can only be so important
in the face of musical magic.
—Graham Nash (Crosby Stills Nash & Young)

Famous for being famous but good at what

The true meaning of the word star is someone that the public takes a shine to. You can be an athlete, a musician, film star or sports person. It doesn't matter as long as you have TALENT. The media today have helped to create this bizarre new creature—the *car-crash* celebrity—the ones who are famous for being famous. They are successfully manufacturing their own *celebrity*, the one they can manipulate and have easy access to. Why, because they made them!

Gone and very soon forgotten

The wannabe will rarely have an agent or manager, or at least one who's any good and knows how to build a career. They become media puppets and do what they are told to do, otherwise they don't get the publicity. It's that simple. They find themselves in a very precarious position because if someone more interesting comes along, they get dumped and are left nowhere and with nothing. That's when they realize who their real friends are and find that those who once were always around are now nowhere to be seen!

Oscar has just left the building

In the past, real talent was acknowledged. You made a good record, people liked you and they waited for you to make the next good record. You proved you were worthy and with the popularity it brought, you became a star. You were judged on merit and on your ability to please and when you became famous you'd earned that recognition. It's the same with actors, those who were especially good won awards and were asked back. The A-list celebrity was born because they were A-list actors. So why do we need Z-list celebrities? Because they're scared shitless of anonymity that's why! They don't know they can't last so they take whatever they can get, a little attention NOW.

Desperation adulation

If that's all you can do and though I can't condone it, I sort of understand. What does baffle me is why talented actors choose that route and expect to come out unscathed. Whether it's bad choices or bad management, don't believe anyone who says *There's no such thing as bad publicity*. That's wrong! There's never been anything good that's come out of a car crash and there never will be. Car crashes are about mangled bodies which is tragic enough. We don't need any more wannabe pile ups.

If you are desperate to get in the papers, you must be very good at falling over, going out without any underwear and always dating men with video equipment. It's the wannabe who is the expert at looking ludicrous.

Wreck and roll

Word of advice—get a good public relation's person (PR) who can protect you from yourself. You'll need it! Everyday, there's another train wreck waiting to happen with the media hungry to pounce. For photographers, the potential cash earned from any photograph they can capture is too big a temptation, what the newspapers will pay for that one picture is obscene. The merest hint of any debauchery or bad behavior, they're in there like a shot. If they don't get the picture, someone else will.

The loneliness of the long distance pop star is something I had to deal with but when you've seen it once it starts to become a pattern. You start to look for it and almost expect it.

The characteristics are the same when it becomes the artist who all of a sudden seems to resent their fame. The classic look of the rock star never changes, the dark cool shades suspiciously hiding the excesses of the previous night. For some they have become a permanent fixture, the ravages of the face no longer wanting to be exposed. It's the ageing rock star disease and it's called *Terminal Excess.*

The morning after

Imagine the scene, beautiful spring morning, early start and a fantastic opportunity for an artist to promote his current single on network television. If only he hadn't gone out the night before, how my life would have been so much easier. In the music business this is seen as preparatory work and something some rock stars do better than others.

He did neither. The sun rose, the singer didn't and I had to wait forty minutes in the hotel lobby with the vague inclination I knew what to expect. Suddenly I heard the familiar ping of the elevator as it settled down in front of me. The doors parted and out stepped someone wearing sunglasses, but it wasn't him. I asked reception to call his room again—no answer. It gets better!

All night surprise

Just as I was starting to get worried, the doors at the front of the hotel flung open and in he came. Surprise! Surprise, he'd been out all night! As if I needed this—a prime time television show that had taken a lot of effort on my part and now, an artist who was less than appreciative.

It makes you wonder why you bother when this is what you get in return. He glanced over and smiled at me. I smiled back, secretly wanting to take him back to his room and throw him off the balcony. At least if he'd fallen I might have had a justifiable reason for canceling the show. No such luck. Better get on with it I convinced myself. This was going to be a very delicate procedure with a very delicate dickhead.

The smell of it all

I waited another five minutes, enough time to swill his beer stained breath away and for him to have a wash. It made little difference that I thought I could get him hosed down once we got to the TV station but it was better than being later than we already were. I had made the mistake of phoning ahead to the TV show's researcher to say we'd be a little late but didn't give a reason or to be more precise, daren't give a reason! *I'll meet you at the front door,* she said in a perky, excitable voice. Before I had the chance to explain the state he was in she'd hung up. *Oh My God,* this was not going to be fun.

A farting of the ways

As I poured him into my car he promptly farted. Thanks a lot! He laughed but I understood. When you're in this state absolutely everything makes you laugh. If I'd told him he was dead he would have laughed. I started the car engine and looked straight ahead out the windshield. Hell, in the time I had spent waiting and dragging him out to the car I'd received a ticket. Now I liked him even less. I didn't suggest breakfast as I'd grown quite attached to the cars interior and wasn't looking for a puke makeover.

The journey from hotel to TV station was exactly seven minutes by which time he had fallen fast asleep and was snoring like a baby. Make that a warthog. We arrived, pulled up and there smiling and expectant was our researcher, Jill. We had reached the point of no return. This was Armageddon!

Sleep useless one

Fortunately, we knew each other well and my smile, together with a wink said it all. *Not a word,* it echoed. Between us we smuggled him past reception as she frantically waved a clipboard at a bewildered commissionaire, all the time looking for the fastest route to the dressing room. Still our baby was fast asleep and then half asleep as his grunts had turned to mindless babble. She draped her right arm around him while trying to prop him up. As if by a gesture of appreciation or just generous affection, again he farted.

By now I had begun counting, the fifth and by far the worse. I'm sure he'd been saving that one up for her. With such a powerful smell he should be dead. She politely reciprocated and gave me a look that said an animal had died on her, two months ago.

Face the music, man

Her face became all contortioned as she winced with pain. As I looked up at her I couldn't contain myself any longer and just cracked up. Bad idea, I lost my grip and dropped him on the floor.

The corridor was clear. Regaining our composure, we lifted him back up and straightened him out the best we could. It wasn't pretty. She curiously asked for my reassurance, *Have I done the right thing?* She was now having doubts about booking him for the show. *Too late now*, I said giving her that confident but slightly disappointing look.

What happened next amazed us both, somehow this cretin managed to perform, but not before an undress rehearsal with a different type of performance. We got him some orange juice and iced water and with a gentle flick across his face, gradually becoming harder, he started to come around.

This was like Frankenstein waking his monster except that this monster looked decidedly worse. Compared to this guy, Boris Karloff looked like a Greek God.

You go through stages where you wonder whether you are

Christ, or just looking for him.

—David Bowie

A mindless wreck

What I later discovered was that he'd been secretly nervous. Getting wrecked the night before was his way of taking his mind off the show. More like taking his mind!

Writing this, I'm still shaking my head in disbelief. It's scary and all too vivid. I slapped him into consciousness and briefed him on what the plan was, call times and so on, and then went off to schmooze with the TV people to get the final run down on the filming. As if I hadn't enough to deal with when I got back to his dressing room—he'd gone! During all his nonsense, I'd noticed he kept smiling and giggling at the make up artist as she was hopelessly trying to apply gargoyle repellant to his face. It kept smudging and he kept asking her to lick it off. It seemed like nothing more than casual flirting as she was giggling too and didn't seem to be offended. I didn't interfere.

Dirty flirty

To work with rock stars you have to think like them. I looked around and sure enough she'd gone missing too. Maybe, just maybe they'd slopped off together.

Suddenly, I heard an all too familiar giggle coming from the back of the make up room, or the appropriately titled *boiler room*. I went over, opened the door—and you can leave the rest to your imagination.

I beckoned for them, well to him, to come out and asked him to do what he was supposed to be doing. *Did I really say that?* I'd been telling him you'll be needed at this time so don't go far and I suppose for him the boiler room at the back of make up wasn't far.

Look out there's a beast about

After all the hard work I'd done in securing a prime-time television show for him, the last thing I needed was a run around from Mr. Shag. It became tiresome but being on the look out came with the territory.

You had to have eyes and ears everywhere. There's no point getting pissed off with them because next time he'll think that taking her back to his hotel is doing the sensible thing—and he'll miss the show altogether. And later on, when I did have a quiet word with him, he told me he'd been nervous. Nervous sex, there's a new one!

I had to deal with managing a kind of nervous sexual tension and then diplomatically, couldn't really tell anyone. I couldn't tell the band's manager, he'd have killed the lot of us. I couldn't tell the floor manager, the girl would have been sacked and I couldn't tell the record company because I'd have my ass kicked for not keeping an eye on him. I didn't dare tell the TV people he'd been out the night before *If only they knew the rest!* And I could hardly tell the girl he was so nervous he needed to have sex with her. She'd be mortified. And thank you for doing it somewhere so I could find you both. It was no surprise that when we did eventually start filming his make up appeared a little rushed.

All that day I'd been thinking why on earth would any girl want to have sex with this? He smelled bad enough from the drink and sweat with his clothes on and surely his flatulence would have played a major role in the seduction. Is this what women want? Whatever his technique, I wasn't going to him for any personal tips on how to woo the opposite sex.

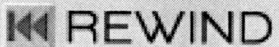 **REWIND**

CELEBRITY

1. **W**onderment: Star-struck is forever the plight of the wannabe, on the outside looking in.

2. **A**ttention: A wannabe will do anything for publicity, whatever that publicity might be. Anything in the hope of everything.

3. **N**arcissism: Has no place in the fame game. Find your own reflection and leave the rest of us alone.

4. **N**UNO: No Underwear on a Night Out: The most popular photo call for the wannabe. Wear it well!

5. **A**nonymity: The greatest fear of all, rejection from attention.

6. **B**onoism: The ability to deal with the glare from both the media and the public. Bono know-how separates the wannabe from The Mega Star.

7. **E**verlasting: The ultimate goal is to retain a legacy, reserved for a select few.

TONY MICHAELIDES

The INSIGHTS COLLECTION was created to provide an insider's view to the stories and lessons learned from the incredible career of Tony Michaelides, one of the most respected record pluggers in the UK. Tony has an irrefutable reputation achieved over thirty-plus years of working with a stellar cast of clients such as: U2, New Order, The Stone Roses, REM, Happy Mondays, The Police, Massive Attack, The Pixies, Bob Marley, Matchbox Twenty, Genesis and Peter Gabriel.

Tony's early years were spent at Transatlantic and ABC Records before moving to Island Records in the late 70's. From here he went on set up his own independent promotion company handling such diverse labels as 4AD, Mute, Circa, Virgin and Factory where he helped set up their regional promotion. He ran his own promotion company, TMP for over twenty years which became one of the most successful promotional companies in the UK. He developed a long-standing relationship with BMG, enjoying their most successful period ever with Annie Lennox, Whitney Houston, Take That, Natalie Imbruglia, Westlife and Puff Daddy and managing, among others Peter Hook from New Order. He spent several years working with the now-legendary Simons: Cowell and Fuller, and presenting his own award winning radio show on Piccadilly/Key 103 in Manchester which he continued to do for nearly 13 years.

1996 marked a personal highlight when Tony was asked to be publicist for David Bowie's *Earthling* tour, responsible for all press, radio and television. The following year, TMP linked to Lippman Entertainment, one of the world's most successful management companies as well as acting consultant to Warner Chappell's LA office and Atlantic Record's New York Office. Tony has achieved numerous awards and consistently worked with the world's biggest selling artists and acts who's sales have been in excess of a BILLION records!

He served as consultant and advisor to *The Music Managers Forum* master classes and became a regular panelist and moderator at the UK's major music conference, *In the City*. He was also one of the founding members of *The Manchester Music City Network*. Mentoring sessions in Canada and the UK continued until Tony moved to the USA after being granted a Green Card as an *Alien of Extraordinary Ability*, a prestigious accolade in itself and awarded only to those who have reached the pinnacle of their careers in music and the arts.

Currently, Tony resides on the Gulf Coast of Florida, where he helps others discover their niche in life as a consultant to various recording artists and music industry organizations. He is a professional speaker who offers his knowledge and insights into the creative process. He teaches the art of management, motivation and the ability to collaborate. He talks about the lessons he learned from rock and roll which are inspirational and motivational, littered with real life stories from the stars he has worked with. For additional information go to: *www.insightscollection.com*.

RECOMMENDED READING

A brilliant book by Graham Jones…. TM

Graham Jones has amassed a fantastic collection of anecdotes on his travels around the record shops of Britain, and Last Shop Standing is a unique slice of social history and record industry folklore. It is also a damn good laugh.

David Sinclair
www.lastshopstanding.co.uk

Last Shop Standing lifts the lid on an industry in tatters. Graham Jones has worked at the heart of record retailing since the golden era of the 1980s. In telling the tale of the industry's sad decline Graham Jones has unearthed wry anecdotes about dozens of rock stars and music industry figures, including The Beatles, Led Zeppelin, Jimi Hendrix, Queen, David Bowie, The Sex Pistols, Joy Division, Oasis, John Peel and many others. *Last Shop Standing* is a hilarious yet harrowing account by a man who has been there and sold that. It is a book that will bring a wry smile to the face of anyone who has ever bought a CD or attended a concert, and still has the T-shirt to prove it.

Hooky at his best…. TM

As co-founder of Joy Division and New Order, Hooky has had a thirty-year career in the music business which has seen him become a well-loved rock and roll icon whose innovative and genre-defining bass playing has driven classics such as *Love Will Tear Us Apart*, *Blue Monday* (the best-selling 12-inch single ever), *Thieves Like Us*, *Regret* and *Crystal*. Peter Hook was also co-owner of Manchester's Haçienda, from its opening in 1982 to the rise of acid house in the late eighties and beyond, and saw first-hand the tumultuous set of circumstances that shaped the club and made it one of the most famous clubs in the world.

The Haçienda: How Not to Run a Club is Peter Hook's indelibly personal memory of that era, and is far sadder, funnier, scarier and stranger than anyone could ever have imagined.   *—Skiddle.com*

Founder of Joy Division, bassist with New Order - myspace.com/peterhook

Fantastic! A totally wonderful book…. TM

INSIGHTS FROM THE
ENGINE ROOM

LESSONS LEARNED FROM ROCK & ROLL

Tony is taking his stories out on the road. The lessons he learned from all those artists are lessons for everyday life—like in the engine room—it's just a different way to look at things. Tony speaks on motivation and interpersonal skills with a devilish sense of humor and a passionate belief, mixed with a zest for life. These inspiring lessons will help you do things that will take you in the direction of your goals and experience the life you have always wanted.

Go to *INSIGHTSCOLLECTION.COM* to see when Tony will be in your area.

INSIGHTS NOTES

CPSIA information can be obtained at www.ICGtesting.com
Printed in the USA
LVOW120952050812

292938LV00001B/2/P